# TWO-MOON POND

# TWO-MOON POND

*by Paul Koepke*

JOHN F. BLAIR, *Publisher*
*Winston-Salem, North Carolina*

Library of Congress Cataloging in Publication Data

Koepke, Paul, 1918–
  Two-moon pond.

  1. Natural history—North Carolina—Durham Co.
2. Country life—North Carolina—Durham Co.
I. Title.
QH105.N8K63    1983    508.756'563    83–6348
ISBN 0–89587-030-4

FOR LYDA, WITHOUT WHOM
IT WOULD NEVER HAVE BEEN

1

# ACKNOWLEDGMENTS

THE AUTHOR WISHES TO EXPRESS HIS INDEBTEDNESS TO the late R. E. ("Cotton") Lee and his wife, Celia, for encouraging him to open his eyes to the world around him.

He also wishes to offer his gratitude to Arthur and Shirley McKneely, Ray and Swannie Haigler and their children, and William and Judy Robertson, who were always there with the buckets when we needed bailing out.

His thanks are particularly extended to Muriel Dyer and Jane Bosman for their assistance in the preparation of this book.

"The Subtlest Beast," "Aerial Anglers," "Big Turkle," "The Dead of Winter," and portions of "Troubled Waters" were first printed by *Wildlife in North Carolina*. Other portions of "Troubled Waters" first appeared in *The Journal of Freshwater*, which kindly granted permission for that material to be reprinted in this volume.

# CONTENTS

After you have exhausted what there is in business, politics, conviviality, and so on—have found that none of these finally satisfy or permanently wear—what remains? Nature remains.

—WALT WHITMAN

I

# Praeludium

Iт's a late afternoon in early November, and a mote-flecked shaft of pale sunlight is slanting through the kitchen window and highlighting the sculptured bird in its nook by the living room door. Once again, as in each of the past seventeen years, the carousel of seasons has come full course, and I am reminded by this heliogram from a southward-slipping sun of the imminence of another alternately icy and soggy southern winter.

The sad old iron bird seems even more downcast than usual today with its head half turned away as if reproaching me for my feckless ways. "Look here," it seems to say sarcastically, "so what if the vegetable garden is tilled and ready for early spring planting? One of these days a norther will come booming across the meadows and the pond, whistling through its teeth and owl-hooting around the eaves, and then what?"

So this mumpish fowl has taken to playing conscience, has it? Well, I suppose it's right; there aren't many mild, sunny days left for us happy grasshoppers, and it's time to be up and doing. Tomorrow, if the weather permits and the fish aren't biting, I will most certainly stow, secure, or batten whatever is out of place, loose, or leaky, have the furnace checked out, and call my genial friend at the woodlot to deliver a pickup load of split ash, oak, and hickory. Those odds and ends of elm, catalpa, and china-berry in the woodpile "ain't got much steam in 'em," as the locals put it, and I can do without any more sidelong looks from my ferrous friend in the corner if my next fireplace effort is a fizzle.

In our time as city cliff dwellers in the North Carolina Piedmont, before we moved out into what our daughter's generation called "the boonies"—and before the bird, who was then just a pair of old automobile bumpers—our maintenance obligations were few and usually involved nothing more taxing than repeated calls to an elusive and grudging building superintendent. But rural living has wrought its changes in us, often by subtle insinuation and sometimes by seizing us rudely by our scruffs and shaking us till our teeth rattled. With chores at every hand, little help immediately available, and Emergency cracking its knuckles in the underbrush, biding its time to uncork another outrage, we have learned to ask not with whom the buck stops: it stops with us.

## Praeludium

We really had no intention of moving to the country. No deep-seated, atavistic urge was pressing us to send down roots in the land; nor did we feel covetously compelled to simply possess property. Our motives were primarily financial. A wise man, Onageras of Boeotia, once said, "The owner draweth sustenance from his benefits, but the renter sucketh a dry teat." Since we had been nuzzling that unproductive nubbin for many years, we finally came to feel that too many investable dollars had been stuffed down a variety of ratholes and so began our search for a small but comfortable house in the city.

But there was one factor, an idle pursuit, which was to alter the shape and quality of our lives in the years to come: both my wife and I love fishing—not as a manic, competitive, first-biggest-most sport, but as an occasional escape from the racket and hubbub of the city to some quiet lake or pond in search of that magic, electric moment when the fly is snapped up, the line jerks, or the bobber slowly sinks from view. This chink in our rational armor proved our undoing, for it made us vulnerable to an ad my wife spotted in the local *Morning Petard* which read, "For sale: 5 room house, 5 acres, 1 acre pond. Call Groatsworth Realty . . . . " A pond of our very own? On impulse, she called.

A few hours later, on a dismal, drizzly February afternoon, we found ourselves on a besotted wretch of a road that had shed its blacktop at the crossroads store and gone lurching and reeling over hill and down dale on its crapulous course to nowhere in particular. Finally, at the top of a rise, the place came into view, and we stopped to take stock. There, across an expanse of water, at the far end of a rutted causeway which followed the top of a dam, lay the property in question: a small meadow with cows, a small tree-sheltered house near the water, several out-buildings, and a neglected vegetable garden complete with dried cornstalks.

We exchanged glances, each filled with a wild surmise which proved to be drastically at variance with that of the other. My wife saw many-towered Camelot surrounded by a deerpark and cool, blue water, over which dragonflies darted in an endless, sunlit summer which stretched to the misty, violet horizon of her imagination. She also stubbornly claimed it would be a good investment. I saw a desolate, late-nineteenth-century, tin-roofed hovel; a swaybacked shed which provided the only visible means of support for a desperate lean-to; a rump-sprung chicken house; sagging, overgrown fences; and several acres of unkempt pasture, over all of which Delapidation brooded like a moulting buzzard. Keeping my voice down for fear that anything over fifty decibels would bring it all crashing down around our ears, I indicated that the purchase of this spread represented the shortest possible route to penury, that we would be cast forth into the snow, that we would feed upon husks, and that this was the craziest idea I had ever heard of. I was as unyielding as basalt. Two weeks later we moved in.

And so began a sometimes maddening but often fulfilling way of life which represented for us not so much a change of place as of focus and rhythm, where the teeming present could be seen with greater scope and clarity and the pulse of the past felt in the beat of a primal drummer far older than man himself.

# II

# In a Little Crooked House

MANKIND, FROM HIS EARLIEST BEGINNINGS, expected one thing above all from his dwelling, whether a cave, a wickiup, a cabin, or a castle: it should keep the more unpleasant aspects of the Great Outdoors where they belong—outside—with admission by invitation only. In this he was for the most part successful, as human presence on earth today will testify, and improved technology and materials have brought him now to the point where he may feel reasonably secure against the milder onslaughts of the elements and the intrusion of all creatures with two, four, six, or eight legs—or none at all, for that matter.

Unfortunately, our newly acquired home proved to be secure against very little. It had sprung from humble beginnings as an unpainted, clapboard tenant farmhouse with three small rooms, a double, back-to-back fireplace, a front and back porch, a garret, and no plumbing. Then, in the early thirties, a change took place. At that time it became customary in this area for a city gentleman of some means to acquire a nearby rural retreat where, on weekends, he and his cronies might drop their cares with their galluses, fish, if a pond was available, and, safe from the disapproving eyes of their preacher and their women-folk, indulge in a few hands of draw poker and a drop or two of the local poteen. And so the little house got a new owner, an acre pond in its front, two more rooms, asbestos siding, electricity, a pump in a brick pumphouse over the spring, plumbing, a forced-air gas furnace of sorts, and a bathroom where its back porch used to be. All this was done so inexpensively and in such a rough-and-not-so-ready manner, however, that the house, while suitable for occasional, short-term occupancy, was guaranteed to give a year-round resident a galloping case of the shaggy hor-rors, and in no time at all we found ourselves so afflicted.

To begin with, the tin roof leaked like a colander, as I knew it would, and we soon became accustomed on rainy days to the asdic ping of droplets in strategically placed pans. Then, one warm April day, we were greeted by a flying circus of swarming termites who seemed healthy and well fed, judging by their dazzling display of loops, Immelmanns, and chandelles. The hastily summoned ex-terminators, though, found their access to the crawl space under the house disputed by a fat copperhead, and so—since one copperhead might indicate the presence of a nest—the termites had to wait while the crew plotted and executed a plan of mass ophiocide. Meanwhile, we discovered that rodents had gotten at the insulated wiring and, as a result, some of the plumbing fixtures, gutters, and downspouts were electrically charged. We were, in fact, living in a leaky, snake-rodent-termite-infested toaster oven.

To add a little topping to our plateful of chagrin, the metal cover which sealed off the stovepipe vent hole in the unused kitchen chimney took to popping off whenever a northeast wind reached fifteen knots or more, showering the table and food with soot and leaving us with the appearance of end men in a minstrel show. Secure that cover as we would, the next northeaster would build up pressure in the chimney, and off the infernal plate would come.

In winter, the wind from that same quarter during a snowstorm would impinge on the slit formed where the main roof overlapped that of the front porch. When the proper wind velocity was attained, it produced what acousticians and organ builders call the edge-tone effect. The eddies formed by this phenomenon created beautifully sculptured snowdrifts in the attic, which we were rarely able to remove before they melted and joined the raindrops in their ceaseless search for sea level.

These leaks and the gnawing termites made common cause, of course, in undermining the integrity of the gypsum-board ceiling, which is why, one night during a thunderstorm, an entire four-by-eight section descended on the head of a house guest, leaving him stunned, cold sober, and thoroughly plastered.

We also soon discovered that we were vulnerable in another area—the water system. Immediately after each heavy rain, our water turned a rich khaki, and it developed that the back meadow drained directly into the spring in the ravine, where the runoff was promptly sucked up by the pump. Since our neighbor's livestock in the meadow were dropping brown berets and tam-o'-shanters with considerable regularity, it was obvious that we were being treated to periodic helpings of cow tea. While this is mother's milk to house plants, it did little for us except turn us a sickly shade of green, so we called the Board of Health. Those worthies took samples, performed tests, and at last advised us that while organisms were indeed present, none were harmful to man and that the only ill effects would be psychological. This was cold comfort to us, since we felt that we were already playing host to all the protozoa we could handle, so we placed the problem in the "Things That Must Be Done" file under "Immediately."

But immediately became by-and-by when that surly beast of a furnace in the dugout cellar got through with us. Actually, for all the British thermal units it produced, it was not a furnace at all but rather a gas-eating, sheet metal octopus whose thumps, clanks, and gut-rumblings kept us constantly on edge. Weekends and holidays were particularly nerve-racking, since it was at these times that our tin pot Fafner chose to doze off without warning, and an ominous silence would prevail. Then, with no heat, the temperature at eighteen degrees Fahrenheit, and the wind nor'-nor'west at twenty knots, it would be necessary to call the local "comfort engineers" to rouse the monster and coax it into operation. This they did, if our ears were any judge, by beating it with a length of lead pipe while offering a nasal rendition of "Beulah Land." Their rites performed, they collected their time and a half and left us to our thoughts and chilblains, while the galvanized cephalopod below fumed and rumbled once again.

All this ended quite abruptly one cold January afternoon when the furnace, in a sudden, venomous outburst, split its firebox with a resounding boom and extended a spiteful tongue of flame to consume the wiring of its own controls. Fortunately, I was there to throw the switches and turn off the gas. Two cases of pneumonia and a flattened wallet later, we had a new heater that really delivered heat and purred like a pussycat.

But there was another kind of feline in the fireplace chimney, a sleeping tiger that awoke one cold spring night with a terrifying roar. A generous buildup of creosote had finally ignited, and the chimney was spewing a shaft of flame like a Bessemer converter. After dousing the fireplace logs and each other, we called the fire company, which arrived in time to witness the denouement. A brief inspection proved that no damage had been done and that the chimney was now as clean as a whistle. Needless to say, we soon found other ways of keeping it that way.

Not so clean, though, was the pink shag carpeting around the stool in the bathroom. The facility itself was, for some obscure reason, mounted on a six-inch dais and illuminated by an impressive lighting fixture immediately above. To this *mise en scène* the carpet lent a certain vice-regal splendor, but we opted for sanitation over status and selected a more appropriate floor covering. It was not until the carpeting was removed that we found, to our horror, that part of the wooden floor and subfloor had completely rotted away and the stool was supported by nothing more than the pipe on which it stood. Why someone temporarily enthroned on this Siege Perilous was not precipitated into the crawl space below in a cascade of plumbing and porcelain fixtures remains a mystery.

All this time our list of needed repairs had been growing like a tapeworm, until it became abundantly clear that the bottom line read, "Total renovation." We had heard, of course, the recurring story, which pops up in this periodical or that, of one or another inexperienced couple who acquired by purchase or inheritance an abandoned ruin of a cow barn which—by working weekends with the help of a local, one-armed, alcoholic handyman—they managed to convert into a Venetian palazzo for a total cost of one hundred and ninety-seven dollars and twenty-three cents. Not only that. They found beneath the moldy straw a beautiful parquetry floor and, in the loft, an exquisite selection of Chippendale furniture and a complete Staffordshire dinner service for twelve. Taking everything into consideration, including the brass-bound casket of gold sovereigns they discovered amid the roots of an ancient oak while planting petunias, they did very nicely indeed.

In our case, things turned out differently. It took a civil engineer–contractor and a hardworking crew three months to produce a tight, plain, comfortable residence, and there was no treasure trove to help pay the sizable bill. Quite to the contrary, the shed was crammed with junk: three thousand cubic feet of *detritus Americanus*, the leavings of three or more generations of human pack rats. As these offscourings were being loaded and hauled away, I came upon one of the few mementos which will be with us always: a glass jug containing a mysterious liquid which fell and broke on the cement floor in front of the workbench. It was greasy, tacky, and stank to high heaven, and, if pressed, I would say it was concocted of cod-liver oil, creosote, and blackstrap molasses. Whatever it was, it resisted all efforts to remove it, and I finally compromised by covering the spot with the old chicken house door on which I now stand when at the workbench.

As for the old chicken house itself, I took it down and sawed the old, unpainted, warped, splintered boards into stove lengths and split them for kindling. It was only when I had thunked the hatchet into the chopping block and picked up the first armload of wood for stacking that I noticed its exposed interior grain and could not believe my eyes. As incredible as it may seem, that chicken house had been built of solid black walnut.

As an alternative to our "enriched" water supply, we hired a well-driller and soon discovered that the original builder had wisely heeded the biblical injunction and had set the house not on shifting sand but on solid granite— one hundred and eighty feet of it. This had to be penetrated (at twice the cost) if water was to be reached, but anything was preferable to the danger of our developing roots and breaking out in a rash of foliage, so we gave the go-ahead and soon enjoyed the boon of cool, clear, sweet water.

With the major impediments to our daily comfort and convenience removed, we were at long last able to devote our undivided attention to the things that had attracted us here in the first place, particularly the pond and the many forms of life that lived in and around it. Once again, however, in some respects, we found ourselves involved in more than we had bargained for.

## III

# Troubled Waters

THERE IS AN IDYLLIC QUALITY ABOUT A FARM POND which causes the passing Sunday driver to ease off on the accelerator and take a longer look. There before him is a scene of pastoral charm, a spread of placid water mirroring the sky. On its surface a flotilla of white ducks sail serenely, and in the green meadows surrounding it a sprinkle of livestock munch their way through the lush grass. To the casual viewer, then, it must seem that the fortunate pond owner is one of the Lord's elect, with little to do but sit on a sunny bank, cane pole in hand, under slowly drifting, castled clouds, fishing and dreaming the happy hours away.

I wish in my heart that this were so, but in this real and earnest life of ours, as Longfellow observes, things are not what they seem. Every man-made farm pond has but one goal in life and that is to become a nice, soggy marsh when it grows up, and it bends its efforts to this end with the aid of all the natural forces available. The owner, on the other hand—if raising game fish is the name of the game—is under constant pressure to remain alert and take whatever measures are necessary to maintain the status quo.

The most persistent agent of destruction is the wind, which impels waves varying from ripples to occasional storm-driven whitecaps against the shore, nibbling and gnawing incessantly at the earthen banks, which eventually crumble, creating shallows. Then, too, heavy rains impinging on any bare ground or dirt road in the drainage area will bring in streams of silt, which settles, producing even more shallow water.

The third menace to the pond's integrity is the unholy trinity of muskrats, livestock, and stray dogs. The muskrats are indefatigable burrowers and, quite aside from the threat they pose to the dam itself, are forever attempting to honeycomb the banks with passageways and underground chambers. The roofs of these, when softened by rain and trodden on by stock, will eventually cave in unless the dogs find the burrow first and attempt to dig out the occupants. This produces even more shallows as well as some small inlets which wave action will eventually widen.

Unless one looks sharply and acts promptly, then, the net result of all this is a shoreline so rutted, uneven, and dangerous that it cannot be kept clear with a tractor-driven mower and shallow water so overrun with cattails, rushes, swamp roses, and various water weeds as to make fishing difficult if not impossible. This shallow-water growth also creates additional problems, for it not only gives shelter to the very forage fish upon which the larger fish are supposed to feed but also, once having died and fallen into the water, becomes essential building materials of a marsh and, in so doing, provides a breeding ground for filamentous algae which, if left unchecked, will eventually cover the entire surface of the pond, rendering it unsightly and useless.

It was into such a situation that we blundered in fatuous innocence when we decided to buy our rural acreage, and since there was no indication to our unschooled eyes at the time that this thirty-year-old body of water was going to pitch any knuckle balls, we drooled in anticipation of warm weather and good fishing.

Spring, however, does not just come to the North Carolina Piedmont; it erupts. After a few warm days and some gentle rain, there was a touch of vibrant, tender green at our feet which gave little hint of the spate of foliage that would come surging up around the pond in the following weeks. By May we realized that we had a crisis situation. All those trifling little sticks, twigs, and canes which had appeared so lifeless and barren in winter had magically burst out in such green profusion as to make it difficult to wet a line. Even worse, as the weather warmed, the pond surface became covered with large floating islands of slimy, line-fouling algae. It was an attractive pond no longer and resembled nothing so much as an abandoned sewage disposal plant. In desperation I called on the county soil and water conservation agent for assistance.

That able gentleman appeared in due time and stared

sourly at me and the overgrown, festering mess spread before us. His name was Jester, but he wasn't kidding. "You gotta keep them edges clean—clean as a swimmin' pool!" he said, in no uncertain terms.

He went on to explain that he had sited the pond and supervised its construction thirty years before and that it was one of the best in the county. It had been bulldozed out of the head of a ravine where the drainage area was adequate but not excessive, thus guaranteeing a full pond in times of normal rainfall and minimal danger of flooding in times of excess moisture. The land itself is well-drained, gently sloping, fine sandy loam with firm red clay beneath, which reduces water loss from seepage. The earthen dam, Mr. Jester pointed out, was particularly well made, and we can testify to its strength and durability for, as a causeway, it serves to this day as the principal access to the property, supporting even a heavy, gravel-laden dump truck without a tremor.

The pond, then, was basically sound and well situated, but years of absentee ownership and neglect had taken their toll, and there was nothing for it now but for us to get cracking. Bidding a rueful farewell to Mr. Jester, my wife and I proceeded to gird our loins and pitch in.

There was no question that clearing off the brush was going to be a manual job. A large portion of the bank and the dam face itself was terrain unsuitable for a tractor-mower, and herbicides were out of the question. Killing off the marginal vegetation would expose the banks to serious erosion, and the herbicides themselves could be harmful to fish and other wildlife.

Tools were required, of course, and in addition to rakes and potato forks, we acquired a fearsome array of cutting implements—bush hooks, machetes, clippers, hatchets, axes, sickles, scythes, and saws.

With the help of a couple of neighbor boys, the great assault began. The most difficult job was removing unwanted brush from the one-hundred-and-fifty-foot ivy-covered dam face, which sloped, sometimes precipitously, into ten feet of water. Since I do not swim, I did most of my cutting sitting down, only to learn that plumping oneself squarely on the stub of a newly snipped blackberry cane can be a very moving experience. After a week of this hacking and shlepping, however, the marginal undergrowth had been removed and the water's edge at last made visible.

What was revealed gave us little comfort. Large clumps of rushes remained in the water, together with beds of stately cattails and an abundance of willow limbs and branches, all intermingled with decaying vegetable matter and the unsightly rafts of green, filamentous algae.

Much has been made of Hercules' cleansing of the Augean stables by diverting two rivers through the area to flush out the residue, but we had no biddable streams at our command and had to rely on elbow grease and stoop labor. The rakes and potato forks were now brought into play, and little by little, roots and all, the tenacious rushes and cattails were loosened and hauled ashore, and large gobs of green, malodorous, slimy gunk were sloshed onto the bank and ourselves, so that by each day's end we looked and smelled like the survivors of an explosion in a spinach cannery.

Fortunately, there is an end even to cattails, rushes, and glop, and the day finally came when we raised our heads as far above hip level as our backs would permit and saw that the edges were at last as clean as Mr. Jester's "swimmin' pool." With a sigh of relief we hung up our tools and turned our charley horses out to pasture. There would be brush to cut several times each year, of course, but the pond would never again be allowed to fall into the wretched state in which we had found it. But, the end was not yet. Although the water was now accessible and fishable, it soon became abundantly clear that the pond was doomed as a source of game fish unless drastic steps were taken immediately. Normally, the pond population should consist of large-mouth bass, bluegills, shell-crackers, pumpkin seeds, and goggle-eyes, all members of the sunfish family. But somewhere along the line some ignorant or careless clot had emptied his bait bucket into the pond, thus introducing a batch of golden shiners into the water and placing the entire operation in peril.

The golden shiner, *Notemigonus crysoleucas*, is a true minnow, which may reach ten inches or more in length. While immature these minnows are highly prized as game-fish bait, and many bait dealers raise them in special ponds for the market, but their presence in a game-fish pond means nothing but trouble. For one thing, they are explosively reproductive and prefer to lay their adhesive eggs on submerged vegetation, which, God knows, we had in abundance. For another, they like to supplement their regular diet of aquatic insects and algae with game-fish eggs and may be seen, in season, ganged up around the bass spawning beds, waiting for the protecting male to turn its back so that they may dart in and gobble up the fertilized roe.

It's not surprising, then, that their rapidly increasing numbers and predatory eating habits put the squeeze on desirable species and eventually crowd them out entirely.

We knew nothing of this infestation at first, but when we began catching nothing but runty bluegills and bass and noticed, on quiet evenings, that the entire surface of the pond was atwinkle with feeding fry, we realized that Old Man Trouble had paid us another visit and it was time to call Mr. Jester again.

As usual, his gate was strait and our scroll well charged with punishment. There was, it seemed, no alternative but to drain the pond completely, kill all the surviving fish, and wait for the rain and runoff to fill it up again. Then we could restock with bluegills and, a year after that, restock with bass. Once again, the cure was almost as bad as the ailment, for it meant that at least four long years would have to pass before there would be anything in the pond worth fishing for. There had to be a better way, and there was.

What I needed was a bait dealer with the help, equipment, and storage facilities to cope with an enormous quantity of live minnows. I finally found him—a huge, burly hulk of a fellow in bib overalls who agreed to "he'p me out." He showed up one morning with a brawny crew, a two-hundred-foot seine, and a large, aerated tank of water on a truck. Heaving and straining, he and his men made a slow, careful sweep of the pond and, in the afternoon, began the painstaking business of transferring the shiners from the seine to the aerated tank with the aid of dip nets and buckets, while returning the desirable species to the pond.

The haul was staggering, as was a subsequent one several months later. The bait man estimated his total catch at one hundred and fifty thousand, which tore a sizable hole in our shiner population and certainly didn't do him any harm. With minnows retailing at that time for fifty to seventy cents a dozen, depending on their size, and allowing for the ones that didn't survive the ordeal, he had "he'ped" himself to seven thousand dollars worth of fish and earned my lasting gratitude.

Chumming with soggy lumps of white bread proved, though, that there were still enough shiners in the pond to bring the population back up to nuisance status in a couple of seasons, so I began the second and third phases of my campaign. Since the number of predatory fish had been seriously depleted, I stocked fifty two-year-old large-mouth bass immediately and fifty more the following year. In no time at all they were tearing the surviving schools of smaller shiners to tatters, leaving only the adults to deal with.

These we removed by the time-honored method of cane pole, hook, and line but with some refinements of bait, tackle, and technique. Shiners' mouths are small and soft, and they tend to pick a worm or cricket to bits without taking the hook. We countered by using the smallest long-shanked hooks available with tiny doughballs for bait. While this made it possible to hook the shiners, landing them was something else again. These fish are sluggish and unresistant in the water, but when suspended at the end of a line, they wriggle and thrash as if possessed, more often than not tearing the hooks free from the soft tissue of their mouths. This problem we solved by pulling the shiner out of the water with a slow, steady, sweeping motion which left it airborne when it emerged. This greatly improved the catch but also increased the chances of being slapped in the chops by a wet and inordinately slimy fish.

My wife and I fished for shiners as often as possible, but progress was slow until we hit on the strategem of luring the neighbor boys into the act by placing a bounty of a nickel a head on this finny varmint, hooks and doughballs provided. That did it. The air was soon glittering with flying shiners, and in a few weeks it was all over. A singleton is still encountered now and then, but in the last twelve years predatory pressure has been enough to keep the shiner population on the brink of extinction. Meanwhile, nobody uses shiners for bait in Two-Moon Pond. Nobody!

It would have been gratifying if we could have eaten all those pests we caught. Their flesh is tasty enough, but those wretched creatures are perverse to the last and contain a number of delicate, Y-shaped bones, any one of which is likely to escape the eye and clog the tubes of the pickiest eater. Instead, we wound up passing them along to a friend, who cut them into generous hunks for use in catching catfish on his trot lines. After all,

> *It's fishbait live, it's fishbait dead;*
> *It has a bounty on its head.*
> *A sorry life, when all is said.*

Though all farm ponds may look very much alike to the casual viewer, each one has a character of its own, and, like a person, as it grows older some traits develop into quirks and cranks which can be aggravated by changing circumstances. This is certainly true of Two-Moon Pond, which has almost reached the half-century mark. Consequently, tending the lawn, garden, and meadow is a strawberry social compared with the task of keeping that acre of water productive, and the problem lies in maintaining good water quality—high fertility and low acidity.

Game fish sustain themselves primarily by preying on other living things—smaller fish, insects, crayfish, reptiles, amphibians, and molluscs. These, in turn, are dependent on smaller life forms, and so on down the morphological ladder to the single-celled algae and plankton which provide the indispensable basic nourishment for the pond's fauna.

Algae and plankton, however, require nourishment themselves, and often this must be provided by regular applications of chemical fertilizers high in nitrogen and phosphate and low in potash. This triggers a "bloom" of tiny monads which, in their billions, turn the water dark green to the point where a shiny object is no longer visible when twelve inches below the surface. This affords plenty of forage for creatures further up the ladder and provides the added benefit of cutting off the sunlight needed by objectionable subaqueous weeds. When the shiny object becomes visible at eighteen inches below the surface, more fertilizer is added, and the cycle begins again. Our pond has an acidity problem since the bottom is sandy and low in calcium. This means performing a periodic test. A reading below 6.5 pH means that fish growth and spawning will be inhibited, and at 4 pH and below some fish will survive but will hardly thrive. If the test indicates a low pH, then, three or four hundred pounds of agricultural limestone need to be dumped into the pond for "sweetening."

Going by the book, this regimen seems simple enough: merely apply what is required as needed, and the rest takes care of itself. Not so. We are completely at the mercy of the weather. The regimen applies to static conditions, but they seldom obtain for an extended period. If the pond is treated at a time when it is near overflow, the runoff from a sudden heavy rain will simply flush a good part of the treated water down the standpipe and dilute the rest. If, on the other hand, a protracted dry spell causes low water, then a similar rain washing through the accumulated manure in the stable yard above us will flush an overdose of nitrogen into the pond, which is retained, producing a banner bloom of those disgusting filamentous algae. Then, too, in a wet season with constant overflow, when fertilizing is useless, the penetrating sunlight will encourage the growth of tall, slender-stemmed pondweed in deeper water, which can only be eliminated by applying an approved pond herbicide. This, unfortunately, will also inhibit the growth of desirable algae and plankton for some time to come and throw the entire fertilization program into a shambles.

All in all, it's the old story of the cooks and the broth; one over-seasons while another dilutes, and a third spills half of it on the floor. But, somehow or other, in spite of it all, the pond continues to sustain three to four hundred pounds of fish at all times, and there is always a good mess handy for the skillet.

IV

# The Magic Mirror

IN THE GROVE, THE MEADOWS, AND THE HEDGEROWS
surrounding Two-Moon Pond Nature plays her cards
close to her vest. These are her silent, secret places which,
except for some obvious birds and insects and an occasional
rabbit or meadow vole, teem with largely invisible life.
Above ground and beneath it, mating, mayhem, birth,
and death run their inexorable course, and not so much
as the trembling of a leaf or blade of grass marks the
emergence of a moth, the spinning of a web, or the sinuous
passage of a snake among the vines. The vegetation itself

responds—slowly, sometimes almost imperceptibly—only to the grosser manifestations of sunlight and dark, the weather, and the rolling seasons. Not so the pond. Held in a hollow in the earth and roofed with a canopy of sky, it is a protean, mercurial mirror that is responsive to every change of light, every breath of ambient air, or any solid which impinges on its surface. No cloud may pass, no raindrop fall, nor any fish rise without the event being transmitted to an attentive witness.

At quiet times when the air is still, the pond reflects to perfection those portions of the sky, the grove, and the surrounding meadows that lie within its scope. It may be steel-gray under an overcast, blue-black under an approaching squall line, or cerulean on a clear, crisp autumn day. It captures with equal clarity the lush green of spring meadow grass, the flame of an autumn maple, or the russet of dried broomstraw and, on cloudless nights, the vault of heaven pricked with stars. As a result, when properly positioned, we are blessed with two of everything, including that great golden moidore of a moon which rose above the dam one night and gave us a name for the pond. But more often than not the pond's surface is disturbed by the wind, and then a million transient prisms transmute the once sharp images into a kaleidoscopic, *plein-air* fantasy of light and color.

Close up, however, at the edge of a quiet, shallow pool, the water is relatively clear, and I may, on hands and knees, observe the slow progress of a water scorpion or a swarm of tiny, new-hatched fry underwater. But if I change my focus to the surface, I find myself instead face to face with the same old nondescript visage which has greeted me in my bathroom mirror for more mornings than I care to remember. Despite the disreputable hat perched on my pate and a pair of gold-rimmed spectacles, there is no question about it: it's me, oh Lord, standing in the need of repair.

I suspect that eons ago among the protohominids this was not the case. It is possible that primitive man at first perceived his reflected image in a pool or puddle as an ill-favored, hostile, mimicking, subaqueous intruder and reacted with grimaces, posturings, and attacks very much as did the dim-witted robin who almost beat his brains out against the shiny hubcaps of our car in a futile effort to send an imagined interloper packing. After countless millennia of this nonsense, evolving man probably hit upon a typical human way of dealing with the inexplicable: if it won't go away and you don't understand it, deify it. This he very likely did, and for ages after, orisons and propitiatory sacrifices were probably offered up to the water goblin to keep it good-humored and well-disposed.

But certainly the day came when one whose bulb burned with a slightly higher wattage than those of his peers recognized in a flash that what he saw on the water's surface was not a temperamental demon but himself—he, Oorg, son of Yorgle!

What a day that must have been for him! Being a little better illuminated upstairs than the others, he probably kept it to himself for a time lest he be stoned for promulgating a heresy and confined himself to returning to the pool frequently for another look. Here he was, seen through his own eyes rather than through the eyes of others, and a very handsome devil of a fellow, to say the least.

But then the magic mirror cast its spell. Handsome, yes, but couldn't he be improved upon just a little? A touch of ocher just so between the eyes, perhaps, or a couple of self-inflicted scars on either cheek? Better yet, a nice, thin, polished bone inserted through the flesh below the nostrils, or even a clutch of feathers to set off the mud-matted hair? The mirror seemed to show its approval as did the peer group who finally caught on to what Oorg was up to, and it was off, heigh-ho, to Vanity Fair.

So maybe it wasn't the snake, the apple, and the woman after all but rather the water's surface which begat Self-awareness which begat Vanity which begat Pride which begat Envy which begat Greed and all the other traits which today characterize civilized human behavior. But if that was really the way of it, it seems the cream of the jest that, having risen from *Urschleim*, Nature's watery slumgullion, his life sustained by water, and with water comprising nearly two-thirds of the flesh that sheathes his bones, man should discover Ego in a quiet pool and forsake Eden forever.

Mirror, mirror . . . .

V

# A Fine Kettle of Fishers

WITH THE APPROACH OF THE VERNAL EQUINOX COMES the initial stirrings of dormant species, and among the first to awaken from its long winter's nap is *Piscator perennialis*, the inveterate angler. Let the rude winds of early March blow as they will, it takes only a nodding daffodil and a hint of tender green on shrub and tree to rouse it from its torpor, and early one frosty morning, as I stand knee-deep in the pea patch, I hear a car door slam in the turnaround and realize that, whatever the calendar may say, spring and the visiting fishermen have come to Two-Moon Pond.

*Piscator* appears in many shapes and sizes and variously equipped. There is, for instance, the old gaffer, complete with spinning tackle, intent on initiating a wide-eyed five-year-old grandchild into the holy rites and mysteries of his favorite folly; or a gaggle of chattering, whooping ladies bearing cane poles; or yet a stern-jawed, compulsive man bearing a sheaf of brand new rods and a massive, deluxe tackle box containing every lure from triple-jointed Wobble-Snockers to glittering, gang-hooked, miniature chandeliers.

But despite this formidable array of predators, the fish are in little peril. In fifteen minutes by Shrewsbury clock, the venerable grandsire's rod and reel will, in the hands of his protegé, become enmeshed in a monofilament web of such incredible complexity that it might well have been woven by a schizophrenic spider.

The ladies, on the other hand, will have their stout cane poles rigged with forty-pound squidding line, navel-orange-size bobbers, and number one hooks loaded with worms and backed by a half-ounce of lead. Setting the bobber for six-foot depth and fishing in three feet of water with the bait firmly buried in the silted bottom, they can be confident of a protracted and uninterrupted discussion of medical and domestic tribulations.

Mr. Compulsive, meanwhile, under doctor's orders to seek rest and relaxation and grimly determined to enjoy himself, will flail the water to a froth with a barrage of bespangled ironmongery. After an hour of frightening the fish out of their wits, he will irritably pack up and tool off in disgust, muttering darkly that the pond is stagnant and void of life.

But for every ten fishermen who know not what they

do, there is one who understands fish and fishing and has, by instinct or trial and error, developed superior skills and methods.

One of the finest fly fishermen I ever met, for example, was a man of middle age who had lost his left forearm in a hunting accident at the age of fifteen. I can only speculate on the vast amount of self-confidence, determination, and patience it must have taken to overcome repeated failure and frustration and reach the point where he could, without the aid of prosthesis, handle a fly rod with skill and accuracy or deftly attach a fly to a tippet with one hand. To see him in action was to witness a living refutation of those whole but self-defeating individuals who choose to hobble through life supported only by the sufferance of others.

Resourcefulness and self-reliance were also the hallmark of a ten-year-old, a quick, sharp chipmunk of a boy of slender means, who made shift with improvised tackle, such bait as he could find, and an often proferred but never accepted nickel which accompanied his polite request for hooks.

He had acquired a sharp eye for any unusual disturbances of the water's surface and could smell a bluegill bed at fifty paces if the wind was right. Wasting no time in plumbing dry holes, he would be quick to find where the action was and, on all but the slowest days, would go whistling homeward with a honeysuckle-vine stringer of fish.

His choice of bait depended on what came to hand on a given day: worms, fatback, grubs, dough balls, crickets, canned corn, grasshoppers, and even, on one occasion, wasp larvae. When I found him one day with a can of the latter, I said, "I don't see any welts on your hide, son. How did you get them?" He dug a grubby toe in the dirt, grinned, and threw me a sidelong glance. "Oh," he replied, "I got my ways."

As the weather warmed and the bluegills began to bed, there would loom on the horizon a certain Mrs. C., a woman of ample proportions, who would come booming down the causeway like a brigantine under a full press of sail and a bone in its teeth. She would be accompanied by her equipment-laden husband, a slender wisp of a man with a tendency to heel over to leeward in the gentlest breeze.

With his burden of boxes, bags, and buckets properly stowed under her command, she would then seat herself gingerly on a tiny camp stool which, like Atlas supporting the heavens, stoically assumed and maintained the burden of the hemispheres, and begin her fishing ritual.

The initial step in her order of service was to line the inside of her lower lip with a generous helping of snuff. This done, she then impaled a lively worm on the hook, and believing, no doubt, that expectoration enhances expectation, heaped insult on injury by squirting a liberal amount of snuff juice on the bait. She then cast in a likely place, raised the cane pole to make the line taut, and then wiggled the tip of the pole, causing the tiny bobber to cut a brief series of antic capers on the water's surface. On the second or third repetition of this ploy the bobber would sink like a stone, and in a minute or two a fat bluegill would be flopping in the bucket. Apparently, the blandishments of nicotine and the epileptic behavior of bobber and bait make an attractive combination.

Shortly after taking up residence at Two-Moon Pond, I became involved in what Sir Arthur Conan Doyle would have called *The Case of the Mysterious Angler*.

In the course of a daily round of the pond edge I found in the grass a six-inch bluegill which had been dried to a crisp in the warm June sun. I assumed that it had simply been overlooked by a visitor and gave it no more thought until the following day, when I discovered that it had been almost consumed, and near it lay a freshly caught fish. Since no one had been fishing in the past twenty-four hours, I was puzzled, and as partially eaten and drying fish continued to appear every few days, I soon found myself inextricably hooked on the barb of curiosity. Some creature with a taste for desiccated fish was frequenting the pond.

My deductive powers, however, are somewhat inferior to those of the inimitable Sherlock, and daily chores made a round-the-clock stakeout impossible. How, then, to apprehend the Mysterious Angler?

It was pure chance that I caught him red-handed. One morning I had crept quietly out of range of Duty's steely eye to do a little fishing myself. While so engaged, I happened to look up and see our dog, Tartan, a half-grown pup of uncertain antecedents, who had been passed along to us by the previous owners of the property. He was standing belly-deep in the water on a narrow ledge which had been formed by wave action on the dam face. This was rather strange since he didn't fancy water much. Slowly his head inched forward and down until suddenly, with a heronlike thrust of his muzzle, he made underwater contact and stood with a nice, flapping bluegill in his jaws. With careful steps he emerged from the water, nonchalantly trotted over to a sunny patch of grass, and deposited the fish.

There it was, then: a fishing dog! It happened that we had just arranged to take him to the vet's for his shots, and while there I mentioned his curious behavior and wondered why a dog who was fed regularly and well would crave a dried fish supplement. The diagnosis was immediate. He had a tapeworm, one of such magnitude that, if stretched out, it would reach from here to Siler City, if not beyond. The proper medication was promptly administered, the parasite exorcised, and Tartan never fished again.

All of which poses an intriguing question. I am no geneticist and, beyond reading of recent experiments involving the genetic transference of learned information in flatworms, have no scientific basis for maintaining that savvy and know-how can be inherited traits among the higher orders. But one thing is certain. Lodged somewhere in the crinkles inside his cranium—together with a strong herding instinct, which was made manifest to our neighbor's livestock and us every morning at daybreak—was the necessary programming that enabled an immature, untaught dog *in extremis* to locate fish and catch them. No mean achievement when one considers that there are many determined, well-equipped, sapient human anglers who come up regularly with nothing.

# VI

# The Fishbait Tree

I HAVE AN OLD FRIEND WHO IS GREATLY RULED BY AN abiding curiosity and a penchant for strange and elaborate enterprises. His fish-cleaning might be interrupted, for example, so that a stomach or two could be opened to determine what the owners had had for breakfast. He performed an autopsy on a newly killed and uncommonly fat copperhead to discover whether it contained live young. (It did.) He hatched a plot to trap a wily fox by employing a new tarpaulin, clean gloves, seven pieces of raw duck for bait, and a snare. For six days, using the tarpaulin for a carpet and the gloves to reduce human scent while handling the bait, he placed a piece of duck on a flat rock near the fox's run. On each of the following mornings the bait was gone. Once again the ceremony was reenacted with the seventh piece of duck, but this time he put the well-camouflaged snare in place. The following morning, to his wonder and amusement, the bait was untouched but instead had received a top dressing in the form of a characteristic pointed whorl of fox scat. Score one for the fox.

So I was past surprising when he told me that he had begun a worm orchard and was planning to market the crop. The orchard, it seemed, consisted of more than a hundred southern catalpa trees (*Catalpa bignonioides*) which he had planted on his rural acreage, and the crop was to be the larvae of the catalpa sphinx moth (*Certomia catalpae*), which fishermen prize above all else as bait for fish of the sunfish family. These worms, he said, feed on the catalpa leaves, are "ripe" when they reach full size, and can then be picked for immediate use or sale, preserved live in cold storage to retard their metabolism and pupation, or quick-frozen for use in off seasons. Having convinced me of the merits of the idea, he handed me four saplings. "Try 'em," he said. "You'll like 'em."

The southern catalpa, locally referred to as the catawba, 'tawba, Chicago [*sic*], Indian bean, or Indian cigar tree, is often planted as an ornamental because of the beauty of its blossoms, but it's certainly not one I'd recommend. Mine caught on immediately and began producing big, heart-shaped leaves, but it wasn't long before I found that each of the trees had become a community center *cum* commissary *cum* hideout for insects of every description. A wide variety of flies, wasps, beetles, bugs, and larvae, including the catalpa worms, found shelter and building material amid the leaves as well as various forms of nourishment, including each other, to the eventual detriment of the foliage.

As the weather warmed, I began to check the undersides of the leaves for the half-dollar-sized blobs of tiny, shiny, whitish eggs which are deposited there by the adult female catalpa sphinx moth, and I wasn't disappointed. The moths performed as expected, and many leaves soon had a closely ordered rank or two of larvae, which crept slowly in reverse, chewing most of the leaf away as they progressed. As they grew larger, they broke ranks, and from then on it was every worm for himself as they spread through the entire tree. With greater size came more voracious appetites, and by July the worms were mature and the trees completely defoliated.

The young larvae were scarcely a half inch long when they hatched and were ivory-colored, with rows of small black dots on their backs and sides. Properly fed, though, they grew rapidly, and in a few weeks, after several molts and the consumption of their own cast skins, some reached as much as four inches in length, and each developed a wide, velvety black stripe down its back and black smudges on its yellow sides. Their heads and posterior horns were also black, except in the case of a few variants which were yellow all over with the faintest of markings.

But not all the larvae made it. Nature exerted its control through a variety of agents which thrived on their victims' substance and materially reduced their numbers in the process. The yellow-billed cuckoo certainly found these ambulatory sausages to its taste, as did an unusual species of snout beetle that stuck its proboscis into the rump of a larva and sucked up its vital juices like cider through a straw.

The most insidious attacks, however, came from what

was to me an invisible assailant, a kind of tachinid fly which laid its eggs in the young catalpa larvae. When these eggs hatched, the tachinid larvae fed on the juices and organs of their hosts and finally emerged through their skins to pupate. This they did by attaching themselves to their victims' skins with tiny buttons of excrescent material and then, standing on end, spinning silken coats around themselves. By the time this unlikely business was completed, many of my worms looked as if they had grains of rice attached to their backs, and each had developed a severe case of the punies. They stopped eating, became sluggish, and finally fell to the ground to decay or be totally consumed, while the attached pupae ultimately produced more tachinids.

The tachinid, though, has its own parasites and, presumably, they theirs, a situation that caused Jonathan Swift to observe in another context:

> So, naturalists observe, a flea
> Has smaller fleas that on him prey;
> And these have smaller still to bite 'em;
> And so proceed *ad infinitum.*

All of which makes for disagreement among those ecological folk who favor natural controls: the tree fanciers tout the tachinids, while the worm ranchers root for whatever plagues the parasites.

As the catalpa larvae matured—and before they had a chance to move down the trees to the ground, burrow in, and pupate—I picked them for immediate use. Unfortunately, the fish seem to adopt a ho-hum attitude when presented with this bait in its natural form, so I resorted to the recommended procedure of pinching off the larva's head and turning it inside out like the finger of a glove with the help of a six-inch piece of baling wire, which must be inserted into its posterior. This messy process, which is guaranteed to revolt the fastidious and the queasy, is not made any more agreeable by the fact that the larvae's bodily fluids leave a deep and lasting yellowish-brown stain on one's fingers and on any clothing they come in contact with.

As a bait, though, these everted larvae are superb. Their exposed body tissue seems to exert a powerful olefactory attraction on the fish, and their toughness and durability make it possible to use one bait for several fish before a fresh one is needed.

After the traumatic defoliation of my trees, I began to have some serious doubts about their survival. As it turned out, I had no cause to worry. No sooner had the leaves disappeared than new buds formed, and by August all the trees had new leaves and a second brood of catalpa worms, which went through the same cycle and met the same fate as the first. As a matter of fact, during the ensuing winter I followed my friend's advice and lopped off all the branches so that the trees would remain at orchard size to facilitate picking. The following spring the trees came back as vigorously as ever. The lopped branches I saved as stobs, sticking some in the garden where, to my chagrin, they took root. Others I stored at the entrance to the lean-to with their butts in contact with bare, damp earth. The following spring they, too, sprouted. It is even said that if a catalpa fence post is set in the ground with the bark on, it will take and sprout no matter which end is up.

Although there may be more than just a whiff of the apochryphal about the fence-post business, there certainly is no doubt about the prodigious regenerative capacity of a tree that can undergo two defoliations and a severe pruning each year and still thrive to provide nourishment for the larvae of a moth which produces two broods a year.

And how did my friend make out with his worm orchard? Well enough, it seems, for the profits are there for the picking, and he nets enough each year as a wholesaler to pay his property taxes. And that beats trying to outsmart foxes.

# VII

## Aerial Anglers

WHILE WE HAVE MANY FRIENDS WHO COME from time to time throughout the year with their spinning rods, fly rods, or cane poles to pit their skill and wits against the piscatorial odds, there are others whom we know only by sight, and they come unbidden on a misty morning, a mizzly afternoon, or in the full, bright shine of a spring day. They do not arrive in pickup trucks or station wagons but rather by air, and they scorn the elaborate battery of tackle most fishermen carry, preferring to do it the hard way with fine-honed talons or a swift and deadly bill.

One of these experts visits us only once a year for a day or two, and about the first of April we begin to watch for its arrival. Sometime during the next two weeks we are sure to spot it wheeling slowly over the pond, see it stall, form its wings into a W, and plummet headfirst toward the surface. At the last possible moment it will brake suddenly, bring its powerful talons forward, and hit the water with an immense splash and flurry of wings. Then it will rise laboriously with a fish in its iron grip, turn it so that it points head forward to reduce drag, and, like a torpedo bomber, head for its temporary hangar in the belt of pines just to the north. It's always an anxious moment for us until it clears the intervening power lines, and its choice of whether to fly above or below seems to be determined by the weight of the fish it is carrying. If the fish is large, the bird will pass below the wires and wait until it reaches the open field beyond before it tries to gain altitude. If the prey is small, however, it will climb immediately and thus be clear of all obstacles.

Once it is out of sight, we breathe a sigh of mixed relief and satisfaction. The osprey is back again, and spring is really here. It will probably return a time or two to feed before taking off for its permanent nesting site, and the few fish we lose to this splendid bird—last year it took three in four tries, an excellent batting average—will never be missed. Besides, we feel that the show it puts on is well worth the price.

An even rarer visitor to the pond is the relatively tame common, or American, egret, which will glide in through the mist like a white spectre, stalk the shallows for a time, and then as silently depart, not to be seen again for months or even years.

Unlike the egret, the great blue heron seems to have much less tolerance of our presence, and the slightest movement on our part is enough to make it stuff its neck back into its shirt, spread its immense wings, and take off for quieter parts. When the pond and yard are deserted, however, it will approach quite near the house, sometimes crossing the front yard near the water's edge as though treading the measures of some antic pavane, pausing now and then to examine the shallows intently for signs of life.

On one occasion a pair of muscovy ducks strayed over from our neighbors' to puddle about in one of the great blue heron's favorite fishing holes. This seemed to cause it some irritation, for with long, implacable strides it moved in on the trespassers. The ducks saw it coming and, with many querulous complaints, began to waddle off in some haste. The female kept going, but the drake—something of an addlepate in my opinion—seemed to lose track of events, forgot what he was about, and stopped to collect what few wits he had.

That was where he made his big mistake, for, as in duckish thought he stood, the heron approached, drew back that long, serpentine neck, and, with the impact of a Roman trireme, rammed him squarely in the sternsheets with his beak. This lesson, applied to the drake's seat of learning, seemed to motivate him marvelously. After appearing to run off in three or four directions simultaneously, he finally took wing, followed by the carping female, who had a few remarks to make about stupidity in general and his in particular. The engagement over, the heron settled down to some quiet fishing in a hole he now had quite to himself.

Some frequent visitors every spring, summer, and fall are the small green herons who, when seen from the rear in silhouette, seem to resemble tenpins but, when seen in profile with necks extended, have gawky, tousled aspects. They too confine their fishing to the shallows near the shore. We can frequently spot one on a late summer afternoon standing motionless and hunched on the bank with its neck completely withdrawn, scrutinizing the water with the nearsighted intensity of a Scrooge examining the account book of some hapless clerk. The only indication of its tension is the continual twitching of its stubby little tail.

The green heron, like the egret and the great blue heron, can strike like lightning, and woe betide the fish or reptile that gets too close. On one occasion we watched as a green heron on the bank struck and captured a small water snake. Some protracted pecking was necessary before the snake quieted down, whereupon the heron, with the blasé nonchalance of a veteran spaghetti eater, proceeded to ingest it headfirst. The snake went down as slick as a whistle except for the tail, which gave a valedictory wriggle before it, too, vanished from our sight. With the snake safely in its crop, the heron shook its head from side to side and shuddered like an old sot who had just swallowed his morning shot of rotgut. The spasm over, it flew off to digest what it had consumed. I hope the process was over quickly. It must be rather disquieting to have one's dinner thrashing about inside.

Kingfishers, those scruffy, devil-may-care divers, are the one species that visit and fish the pond year-round. At any time between sunrise and sunset, winter or summer, you may hear one rattling its ratchet from the mimosa tree at the pond side or see it land on a pasture gatepost near the water. For the most part, it prefers to make its dive from a considerable height and a stable perch, although I have seen one hover in one spot in midair for as long as five seconds before beginning its descent.

Like the osprey, it hurls itself bodily into the water to make a catch, but unlike the osprey, it has no talons to use and has to rely on a beak that is of formidable proportions when compared with the size of the bird itself. Despite what would appear to be a rather cumbersome piece of equipment, however, the kingfisher is well named. All this awkward diving and clumsy thrashing about in the water usually culminates in a completed catch and a bedraggled, sodden kingfisher, fish in beak, flying off to a suitable perch where it can prepare its dinner properly.

A kingfisher does not swallow a fish immediately after catching it, as the herons do. Rather, it prefers to have its prey dead and limber, and to achieve this it flies to the near pasture gate by the pond and proceeds to whomp the fish on the top rail with great vigor and persistence until it reaches a satisfactory state of quiescence and flaccidity. That done, the fish is turned headfirst and goozled in a flash. It was not until I witnessed this operation that I realized why the top rail of the gate always has a generous dressing of blood and fish scales on it.

Ponds in this area seldom freeze over, but when they do, it is bound to create problems for water birds. We often wondered how the kingfishers, for instance, survived a week or two of frozen conditions, but the question was answered one bitter January day when my wife, out tramping the road, spied one perched and rattling in a tall tree near a ditch. Suddenly, from that great height, it dived into the shallow trickle of a spring-fed rivulet and came up with something to help tide it over till better times. Apparently, if there is moving water with life in it, a kingfisher will survive, come frost or freeze.

There are other birds that fish our pond from time to time, but their fishing activities are less spectacular and flamboyant than those of the ospreys, herons, and kingfishers because they are conducted, for the most part, under water. Besides, these birds come with no regularity at all and seem to show up at our watery motel only when benighted or blown off course during migration. Then they will stay a day or two to recuperate before continuing their long journey to wherever. Thus, after a stormy night, it is not unusual to find a common merganser or two, a pair of buffleheads, or a pied-billed grebe swimming about on the pond and diving for a small bluegill or bass.

And so they come and go, these airborne fishers, lending the elements of variety and enchantment to our daily lives while keeping their vital place in the scheme of things.

# VIII

# *Requiem for a Duck*

ONE PLEASANT EVENING AS I SAT QUIETLY VEN-
tilating my adenoids and supervising a better-than-
average sunset, I was interrupted by a phone call from my
old friend of worm orchard fame. He had, it seemed, a
duck—a male mallard with an injured wing—which he'd
found walking the city streets near his house. He had
taken it in, given it a drink, and was now trying to provide
it with a foster home. We had a pond, he said, and one
duck wouldn't be much trouble. Would we take it?

This gave me pause. After our experience with our

neighbors' pair of dopey, messy, meddlesome Muscovies, we had come to prefer our ducks well done with orange sauce. But my friend was the soul of kindness and we hated to turn him down, so we gave the nod, and in less time than it takes to say *Anas platyrhynchos* there he was at our doorstep with his rather disheveled and out-of-sorts charge. On the spot we christened it Robert, after its savior and benefactor, and released it near the water, which it took to as the time-honored cliché says it should.

Robert seemed to be content at the pond, and after his summer molt was completed, he proved to be as handsome as other drakes of his kind. Unfortunately, he was not as well endowed intellectually, as his inability to adjust to changing circumstances indicated.

We had begun putting corn out for him at a specific place and time, but as winter came on we moved the feeding place a few feet so that we might observe him more easily as well as the thieving starlings who often made short work of his provisions. His response to this earth-shattering innovation was to come waddling straight through the corn spread for him, stand in the original feeding spot, and quack his head off for nourishment. We even tried to wean this resplendent clabber-head away from his old habit by scattering a little feed at the old place and dribbling a trail of kernels to the new spot where the corn was laid on with a lavish hand. Thus led by the nose he usually managed to find his food, except for the occasions when the starlings got there ahead of him and ate up the trail. Then, remembering nothing, he'd be back at the old stand complaining loudly.

As spring approached we conceived the notion, probably erroneous, that Robert might require some feminine companionship. Allowing our normal prudence to be swamped by a wave of sentimentality, we began to explore the possibilities of providing him with a consort. An ad in a farm bulletin advised us that the school of animal husbandry at a nearby university had a female mallard in need of food and lodging. We made inquiries and discovered that, although she had been the subject of certain laboratory experiments and looked slightly odd, she was in good health and might be just what we were looking for. Without further ado we went to pick her up, accepted delivery sight unseen in an appropriate container, and took her home.

It was not until we released her at the pond side that we got a good look at our new boarder. "Slightly odd looking" was putting it mildly; she was downright grotesque. It seemed that the lab experiments had dealt with skin grafts, and this particular subject had had a piece of her scalp lifted and turned one hundred and eighty degrees. The graft had taken, and the feathers grew, but in a direction opposite from that of the rest of her plumage. As a result, Celie—whom we had named after the wife of Robert's godfather—was endowed with a crest like a worn-out shaving brush, which gave her a rather frowsy and befuddled appearance. But if we were surprised, Robert was utterly confounded. To have another duck suddenly appear, and a weird-looking female at that, was enough to send him squawking and flailing down the pond in bug-eyed consternation.

But Robert, while not big in the brains department, did have a few normal instincts rattling around in an otherwise empty head, and in the inevitable nature of things it was not long before he, the grand seigneur, took Celie in tow and began to show her, with considerable smugness, "his" pond, "his" dabbling places, "his" corn, and "his" obedient serfs who toiled so diligently on his behalf. She was evidently impressed by what she saw, and the pair soon became inseparable.

Things went along smoothly enough for a few weeks until Celie began to behave peculiarly. Instead of swimming dutifully behind her dim-witted liege lord, she took to sashaying around the edges of the pond and laying eggs with gay abandon whenever she took the notion. Once the eggs were laid, she took no further interest in them nor in the hutch I had built for her, and soon we were having fresh duck eggs for breakfast.

But after a week or two of this fiddle-faddle, Robert, who thus far had ignored her strange behavior, intervened, got her into the water, and seemed determined to drown her if at all possible. Knowing little of the ways of waterfowl, I reported this curious event to my farmer friend, Lester Pedeza. "What's going on?" I asked. Les stared at me for a moment in mute incredulity, rolled his eyes heavenward in an apparent plea for divine guidance, and finally explained to me in the simplest of terms that this was the way big ducks made little ducks and to pay it no mind. Sure enough! In a short time Celie had built a well-hidden nest under a bower of blackberry canes some distance from the pond and was proudly ensconced on a clutch of eleven eggs.

Robert dissociated himself from these proceedings except to call her for dinner each evening, at which time she would waddle down to the feeding ground, gobble a hurried meal, and traipse back to the nest. It was beginning to look as if we were going to have mallard ducklings whether we wanted them or not.

Our apprehensions, as it turned out, were unfounded. Our vacation time had come, and leaving the feeding in the hands of a reliable neighbor, we took off. The first day after our return we became convinced that things had gone sour. Robert's calls to dinner went unanswered, and there was no sign of Celie. I cautiously checked out the nest and drew a blank: no eggs, no shells, no feathers, no Celie.

Robert was not himself after Celie's mysterious disappearance. He seemed to wander about aimlessly and continued to call at dinner time with no results. He was in molt now, and this, together with his injured wing, made flying impossible. As for swimming, the summer had marked the appearance of two large snapping turtles in the pond, and he at least had sense enough to steer clear of them. And so he was land bound and vulnerable, a literal sitting duck.

The final blow fell one morning when a neighbor boy who was fishing came to tell me that there was a dead duck at the edge of the pond. He showed me the spot, and there lay Robert, or what was left of him. Not a feather was ruffled, the wings were carefully folded in place, but he had no head nor neck. He had been neatly decapitated, and at the point where the neck had joined the body there was only a rosette of gray feathers with a small crimson spot in the center—a macabre little flower.

Who was the grim headsman who dispatched Robert? All the smart money at the barber shop says "Mink," and that's as good a guess as any. But one thing is certain. Death stalks the darkling hedgerows and grassy pond sides, and waterfowl live a chancy existence at Two-Moon Pond. There'll be no more ducks for us.

## IX

# Come and Get It

EXCEPT FOR MY BRIEF STINT AS A HASHSLINGER, potato-peeler, and pearl diver in a greasy spoon during the Great Depression, neither my wife nor I had had any experience in the restaurant business other than as paying customers. It was not until we came to Two-Moon Pond that we found ourselves with many hungry mouths to feed and became, from late November to early March of each year, the owner-operators of an open-air free lunch stand. We serve twice daily, and each morning and late afternoon one of us may be seen with a bucket of goodies and a gob of glop while the free-loaders gather from far and near for the handout.

Our clientele is a rowdy, fractious crowd who prefer to dine *alfresco* and with little regard for the sanitary code. They kick the food to the ground and walk on it while eating, and since the edibles their neighbors are consuming usually seem more appetizing than what is immediately before them, they fight their neighbors for food, often obtaining by assault or intimidation what they cannot gain by stealth.

In the usual course of human events such behavior would justify calling the sheriff, but in this case it lies outside his jurisdiction, for the perpetrators of these particular misdeeds are not people engaged in their usual social intercourse but birds, whose activities, unless performed by large, noisome aggregations, are not subject to the law's displeasure.

Our reasons for not only tolerating but encouraging this daily Donnybrook involve not only the pleasures of observation, which we share with other bird-lovers, but certain practical and altruistic considerations as well. The birds we feed, whether locals or migrants, have spent the previous spring, summer, and fall ridding us and others of weed seeds and insect pests, and we feel justified in providing these seasonal workers with a kind of unemployment compensation to tide them over hard times. Furthermore, these gratuities sometimes encourage native species to nest close by, giving us the benefit of their services when the weather warms; and as far as the migrants are concerned, we have the satisfaction of knowing that the white-throated sparrows, juncos, and evening grosbeaks will return again to their home breeding ground in reasonably good condition.

Since the bird population at Two-Moon Pond is dense,

we long since gave up using any of the many varieties of feeders commercially available and set up a feeding station which affords the greatest access to the greatest number. It consists of nothing more than a pointed, seven-foot cedar post sunk into the ground. Attached to it at a height of three feet are three trenchers made of hollowed-out cedar log halves, which serve as seed feeding troughs, and above them, randomly placed, five one-inch holes were bored. These holes are filled with a malleable, noncrumbling mixture of birdseed, cornmeal, peanut butter, and fat, and three of the apertures are provided with perches to accommodate birds of that preference, while the other two are more or less intended for the woodpeckers and sapsuckers for whom perches are merely an obstacle.

We soon discovered, however, that the seeds in the trenchers flew in all directions under our patrons' feet, and so, bowing to their lack of social graces and the law of gravity, we now simply scatter the food on the ground as though we were feeding chickens. So far, since squirrels prefer the more forested areas and are therefore not a problem, everyone gets served, and there have been no complaints. The mourning doves, sparrows, thrashers, towhees, cardinals, finches, meadowlarks, blue jays, evening grosbeaks, and juncos take it in their stride. If it rains and the seeds get wet, they eat them anyway, as they have all their lives. A light snowfall is soon trodden away under thousands of little footsteps, and if the fall is heavy, some bescarved and bemackinawed clod is bound to appear periodically with a broom to police the area and provide more grub.

And so, each winter morning and afternoon when the feed is put out, our backyard erupts into a williwaw of feathered confusion. The dominant group consists of nine blue jays who rule the roost for a time in the morning but rarely show up for the late afternoon spread. A dozen mourning doves always appear but first take the precaution of sending in one of their number, who is either the intrepid leader or the low man on the pecking pole, to case the joint and reassure those who follow. Several dozen cardinals assemble, with as many as a dozen feeding at one time, and a cloud of weaver finches, white-throated sparrows, juncos, song sparrows, and field sparrows dart in and out of the melee, grabbing what they can when the larger birds are distracted. Meanwhile, the titmice, the chickadees, and the feisty pine and myrtle warblers flicker through the interstices and eat on the run. The towhees, on the other hand, prefer to approach on foot and kick free the seeds that are hidden in the grass. The nuthatches, perversely enough, seem to feel that if it can't be done upside down it's not worth doing and so begin at the top of the post and work their way down headfirst. The real heavy in all this motley crew, however, is the male red-bellied woodpecker (the belly of which is actually a kind of pinkish apricot), whose formidable bill entitles him to anything he wants, whenever he wants it.

Squabbling between species is continuous and mainly nonselective; but real, overt discrimination is shown by male woodpeckers and cardinals toward their own females. How much of this is a display of macho dominance and how much is concern for the maintenance of the females' trim, sylphlike figures is hard to say, but most certainly, as with humankind, when the urge to mate comes around, these same males will court the females most sedulously and pose as the very souls of solicitude.

As far as brashness is concerned, the smaller the bird, the bolder it is. At feeding time it is the chickadees, titmice, and warblers that natter and swirl around our heads. The larger the birds, the farther they back off when we appear. As for the chickadees, they seem to be constantly sending in Morse code, and the commonest letter is "• • • -," a V. Why a V? For victory? Over what? Or are they Beethoven buffs with a fondness for the first movement of his fifth symphony? Or yet again are they little winged messengers of destiny employing this *Schicksalmotiv* to remind us of our mortality? Nothing so profound, I suspect—just an expression of impatience in chickadese.

Only one group of birds is unwelcome, and that consists of the combined forces of starlings, cowbirds, red-winged blackbirds, and grackles. They descend in a sooty, eddying swarm on the feeding area and in no time pick it as clean as if it had been carefully vacuumed. In vain do we clap our hands and wave our arms. They retreat only as far as the nearest tall tree, clucking, burbling, and gracking and keeping a sharp lookout. As soon as our backs are turned, the sable scourge returns. The only benefit we derive from their presence is that our maledictory vocabulary is kept keen and bright through constant use.

In previous years we had a rather strange visitant whom we dubbed El Bandido because of the black mask across its eyes and the fact that it was easier to say than "loggerhead shrike" or "*Lanius ludovicianus.*" We had our first intimation of its presence when the branches of our honey locust tree began to bear strange, grim fruit. Impaled on its long, sharp thorns were the following: the goozled-out abdomen of a large grasshopper, one June beetle alive and kicking, one small frog entire, the front half of an assassin bug, a fragment of what appeared to be mole skin with a gobbet of flesh attached, and a wing and part of the fuselage of a weaver finch. Clearly, a so-called butcher-bird was in our midst and thriving. When winter came, it lurked around the fringes of the feeding area without molesting the guests, and rather than freeze it out of the action, we began impaling chunks of suet on the tree, which it consumed with considerable gusto. In this it was soon joined by the red-bellied woodpeckers who, being unable to perch on the slender twigs, chose to dangle by their toes while feeding upside down.

Because of its feeding habits, the shrike receives a very bad press from those inclined to anthropomorphize. In fact, the title, *The Shrike*, was given to a Broadway production and a motion picture that dealt with the misdeeds of one of the nastier characters in dramatic literature. But the bird itself is locked into a situation over which it has no control. For a carnivore and insectivore its physical equipment is peculiar. Its large head is supported by a short, thick, strong neck and bears a heavy bill for ripping and tearing. Its legs, on the other hand, are the spindly ones of a perching bird, and the sharp talons of a bird of prey are completely lacking. Obviously, in such a situation as this, a meat hook of some kind on which to impale its prey becomes a *sine qua non*, and to damn the pot is to damn the potter.

On several occasions when on my hands and knees in the garden I have become conscious of the shadow of great wings passing slowly across me and experienced an involuntary flash of spine-tingling alarm from some neural network as old as anything that ever walked or flew. In each case it was only a turkey vulture which swept lazily on after discovering that I was still alive and not yet ripe for plucking. But suppose it had been a fierce bird many times my size who moved like lightning and preferred its prey alive, alive-oh?

This appalling thought gives me some understanding of the skittishness of the birds at our feeder, for this is the threat they live under constantly. Our sharp-shinned hawks have been replaced by a pair of their larger cousins, the

Cooper's hawks, and even birds the size of mourning doves now live in perpetual peril. The Cooper's hawks like to sweep down out of the sun in the early morning or, on gray days, to ease from tree to tree prior to a sudden, slashing attack. It's the talons that do the killing, after which the hawk will stand grasping the carcass and surveying the area. Then comes an almost perfunctory and seemingly ritual plucking with the beak to determine if the prey is indeed dead. One or two puffs of feathers fly, and the hawk takes off with its prey and disappears.

I never interfere. Hawks killing doves is an essential part of the natural order of things, and the application of quasi justice out of maudlin compassion can wreak a havoc of its own. Consequently, with the coming and going of birds and winters there will always be a morning when I find in the grass by the feeder a little, feathery graffito which reads, "*Accipiter coóperii* was here."

With the end of the winter feeding period the cedar post is drastically altered in appearance but not in function. Each spring I fit it throughout its height with a chicken-wire collar and plant a ring of cardinal climber seeds at its base. In a couple of months a homely post has been transmuted into a pillar of feathery green leaves and cardinal red trumpets, to the delight of the hummingbirds who nest nearby. Then, in autumn, with the hummers on an extended holiday in southern Mexico, I will harvest the vine seeds and remove the wire collar and frost-nipped vines in preparation for winter and another onslaught by our hungry, aerial hooligans.

# X

# Curiouser and Curiouser

THEY TELL ME THAT MANY YEARS AGO WHEN I WAS
quite young I could often be found in our urban
backyard in pleasant weather staring by the hour at ant-
hills, ant-lion larvae pits, and spiderwebs. It is difficult
at this distance in time to recapture the wonder I must
have felt when the world was brand spanking new to me,
but I do dimly remember offering the bustling formicids
newly swatted flies and watching the ensuing organized
confusion. I also recall that sometimes, more in mischief
than in experimentation, I would disturb the sand on the

hill or pour water down the hole just to see them scurry, and I must confess that, like nasty little kids the world over, I would occasionally drop a live ant down a doodle-bug's funnel or a live cricket into a spiderweb to get a glimpse of the fearsome proprietor.

Fortunately, my penchant for playful cruelty was short-lived, and in a year or two I became involved in collecting moths and butterflies and sundry live, wriggling horrors, including a big, fat, green, spiny caterpillar, which I caged and fed with oak leaves until it pupated and one day emerged to cling to my bedroom curtain—a magnificent polyphemus moth. My mother managed to keep the damper of patience on her smoldering disapproval throughout these trying times until the day when she discovered the empty jar in the pantry which the night before had contained six perky salamanders. All zoo-keeping ceased forthwith.

But they were not long, these golden, sunny afternoons, for I soon grew up and passed through the looking glass to spend the next half-century in hot pursuit of this *ignis fatuus* or that. It was not until we were settled in at Two-Moon Pond that I felt the tug of cords I thought had been long since loosed and found myself leaning on my hoe handle to observe once again the curious behavior of living things around me.

What was stirring in me, of course, was curiosity, and it sprang from a desire to understand a little more of nature so that I might better determine my own place in it. Here I am, after all, creeping about on a little spinning pill that revolves around a star in an unthinkable immensity of space and sharing its surface with a myriad of life forms, comparatively few of which happen to be of my own kind.

Mine is not the curiosity of the scientist, though, since I lack the training and facilities for research, nor is it that of the dedicated naturalist, for I lack the kind of admirable patience and fortitude that would allow me, for example, to conceal myself for hours in a mosquito-ridden marsh to witness the mating display of the tufted bungstart. For my part, I am served well by a serendipity that complements my slothful nature, and as Nature is notoriously fickle in bestowing her favors, the idler may well stumble upon what the dedicated investigator seeks in vain.

And so I observe and later speculate on what I have witnessed—not at my desk with pen and paper but rather in the garden with a hoe, inasmuch as I discovered long ago that my creative mechanism seems to be located in my posterior, for it switches off automatically the minute I sit down. In the dull routine of weed-beheading I can relive the experiences and juggle this phrase with that until my thoughts become clear and something resembling coherence emerges. And sometimes, while mulling and chopping, I get another peek behind the curtain.

Imagine poking about in a tangle of sweet potato vines, as I was doing one day, and finding on a green leaf a small beetle one quarter-inch long that appeared to be fashioned of solid, glistering gold. Gleaming in the sun and exquisitely made, it might be taken at first glance for a once-treasured bauble of some long-dead Nefertiti. It was no scarab, however, but rather, as I discovered later, a golden tortoise beetle, *Metriòna bìcolor*. As the Latin nomenclature implies, the beetle is not normally golden but rather a dull, reddish brown. It has, however, the biochemical capacity to turn golden at will, although in death its luster fades, never to return.

Here's a puzzle. Adopting protective coloration to match the background as the chameleon does is one thing, but to turn a shining gold seems to be asking for attention, if not trouble. Is it a sexual attractant, a result of sheer exuberance, or a display of plain vanity? But now I'm anthropomorphizing. Is it possible that this beetle's potential predators do not perceive the color gold as humans do, or do they associate it with an unpleasant flavor or with emetic properties? Or, at last, do they realize, along with Midas, that, however attractive the stuff may be, gold is indigestible?

In addition to gardening and indulging in creative otiosity, I served for a time as a voluntary caretaker of a seven-acre piece of woodland adjoining Two-Moon Pond which was the property of an absentee owner. Every now and then I would amble through it, checking in season the ferns, wild iris, fire pinks, and alumroot, as well as the wild cress in the streamlet by the spring, and keeping a sharp eye out for a glimpse of the resident woodcock. On one of these strolls I spied a lightwood stump, a pointed, resin-impregnated remainder of a long-dead pine, which rose like a stalagmite from the forest floor, and I thought it would be just the thing, when split up, for quick ignition in my fireplace. I wiggled it and, finding it as loose as an outworn milk tooth, gave it a hearty jerk. Out it came, and out also came a panic-stricken female woods rat with two small, hairless, purple offspring, one clinging desperately to each flank, and bouncing like saddlebags as she dashed madly off into the underbrush.

I had my lightwood but did not care much for my inadvertent role as the surly bailiff, the brutal evictor of widows and orphans. This self-recrimination lasted about ten minutes, by which time I had convinced myself that I had merely been another of nature's instruments, a kind of involuntary, two-legged tornado that raised the roof and brought the walls tumbling down. I could have put the stump back, but I seriously doubt whether things would ever again have been the same at the old homestead.

What I wonder about are the little sucklings clinging to their mother's flanks. They certainly couldn't remain there constantly, for they had to nurse, and I'm sure she didn't want them on her back twenty-four hours a day in any case. The chances are that somewhere between my wiggle and my heave they climbed aboard and clung like burrs in anticipation of whatever might ensue.

One of the most astonishing things my wife and I witnessed during our time in residence was a small creature swimming furiously down our pond against a crosswind. It was taking a diagonal course across the water from the grove in the northwest corner to the clear bank on the southeast, and we stood stock still until it reached land and crept ashore. We approached cautiously and found ourselves gaping at a soaking wet and completely pooped chipmunk, which, by my calculations, had just swum four hundred and fifty feet. We withdrew but kept it in sight until it got its wind back and scurried to the shelter of the big forsythia.

My guess is that it had felt itself to be in dire peril—I suspect from a neighbor's cat—and was determined to put as much water between itself and the danger as possible. Actually it was in greater jeopardy than it may have realized for, drowning aside, it could have wound up in the crunching jaws of a snapping turtle or in the gaping maw of a big bass, which could have gobbled it down very readily indeed.

A similar event took place one afternoon when I found myself in the company of our neighbor's dog. Trigger he was named, but quick he was not, either mentally or physically. We were half adoze in the shade that afternoon when a rabbit appeared on the causeway. The rabbit was unaware of Trigger, who spotted it at last and finally decided that, being a dog after all, he needed to investigate. After some effort, he managed to get all four legs under unified command and approached his quarry with great deliberation. He was almost upon it when the rabbit became aware of his presence and gave a mighty leap off the dam into ten feet of water. I assumed that it was goodbye Uncle Wiggly, until I realized that the rabbit was quietly swimming along under the overhanging foliage at the dam's edge to disappear at last in the protecting ivy on its face. Trigger, meanwhile, was carefully scanning the skies for flying rabbits.

I had noticed a difference in the rabbit's tail before it took off into the pond. The common eastern cottontail has a scut which suits its name, but this one's was bluish-gray. A riffle through my field manual set me straight. This was a marsh rabbit, *Sylvilagus palustris*, a dweller in swamps and marshes and an able swimmer. Ours undoubtedly lived in the marshy thicket in the ravine below the dam. One of its kind may have caused that flurry in the press when it "attacked" President Carter on one of his fishing trips.

And so, like that little boy in the city backyard, I still encounter things both strange and intriguing and have plenty of grist for my speculative mill. Curiosity, they tell me, has killed its share of cats, but I hope it will spare me yet awhile. I'm afraid I'm hooked.

XI

# The Subtlest Beast

EVER SINCE EDEN, WHERE, ACCORDING TO GENESIS, God cursed that most subtle and guileful creature, the serpent, for its part in the corruption of Adam and Eve and commanded it to crawl forever on its belly in the dust, snakes have stood in a curious relationship to man. They seem, somehow, to have become associated with evil, madness, and horror, and even today, as everyone knows, the hidden assailant is a snake-in-the-grass, the liar speaks with a forked tongue, the ingratitude of human offspring is more keenly felt than a serpent's tooth, and the snake's sinuous form glides malevolently through the feverish visions of the delirious.

Everyone is entitled to his phobias, of course. There are those who hit the panic button when a cat appears, those who claw the walls at the sight of a spider, and I even knew a girl who was reduced to blithering idiocy when she found herself in the same room with a fluttering moth; but human fear, hatred, and loathing of snakes is so nearly universal as to make me wonder sometimes if it is not bred into the bones of most of us.

There are parts of the world, to be sure, where venomous snakes are a part of daily life, and the natives would never dream of popping their corks when a snake is sighted. They simply accept the krait, ringhals, fer-de-lance, or black mamba as one of the less desirable aspects of their environment and have been taught to conduct themselves with due caution in snaky environs. But many North Americans who have never been in anything wilder than a rose garden and have never encountered a poisonous snake in their lives will turn into a pillar of gelatin if a garter snake rears its head. So deep-seated are these largely unprompted and untaught feelings, in fact, that the first action taken by many, if fear is mastered, is to kill the snake, regardless of its species. As a matter of fact, the average motorist, who would swerve to avoid a dog, cat, squirrel, rabbit, or even a Norway rat, for that matter, grasps the wheel firmly when a snake is sighted on the road and steers to kill no matter what kind it is. Apparently, "A good snake is a dead snake" is one of the unspoken mottoes of our time, and most citizens feel only that they have done their civic duty by giving a harmless corn snake a taste of steel-belted radials, to the eventual detriment of us all.

There is a wide variety of snakes in the North Carolina

Piedmont, and we have our share at Two-Moon Pond. Without a doubt the most attractive of the lot is the rough green snake, *Opheodrys aestivus*, that weaves its way through the honeysuckle vines behind the shed and blends so well into the twisted tangle that it is absolutely invisible to the casual passerby. Only people like myself who are given to slouching about in slack-jawed meditation are likely to detect a movement of light, bright, enameled green among the leaves, which could not be caused by the wind. It's a gentle creature, and we always let it go about its insect-eating business.

Snakes tend by nature to be a secretive lot, and we seldom see the terrestrial varieties unless we deliberately go looking for them or something happens to alter their environment, such as the introduction of cattle into the meadow after months of no grazing or the mowing of hay for baling. Then they seem to get stirred up and may appear in our lawn or be observed creeping along on top of the matted, new-mown hay. Heavy rains sometimes flush them out of their hiding places in the ravine as well. In these instances we usually take pains after dark to watch our step in the event that our sole venomous variety, the copperhead, might be abroad and hard to detect.

The one snake that maintains relatively high visibility, however, is the incredible black rat snake, *Elaphe obsoleta / obsoleta*, which seems to be quite careless in the way it exposes itself. No spring would be quite complete without a couple of them slithering across the lawn to the accompaniment of noisy, dive-bombing mockingbirds. They seem to be indifferent to the approach of humans and usually pursue the even tenor of their way even when you stroll along beside them.

The most remarkable aspect of this particular species is its fantastic ability to climb almost anything that has a rough surface. On several occasions one has entered our shed through one of the many crevices in the walls and worked its way up to the top of a ten-foot support post in the southeast corner, where it curled itself up comfortably to sleep off and digest whatever it was that bulged like an indoor baseball in its middle. Several individual black rat snakes have used this spot for that purpose, so the news of its location must be getting around somehow.

Access to the top of the post is not the easiest thing in the world for a snake to accomplish. The first six feet can be quickly achieved by means of a heavy bracing beam which runs up from the floor at a forty-five-degree angle, but the next four feet is absolutely perpendicular and doubly difficult on a full stomach, I should think. Nevertheless, the black rat snakes seem to consider it no big deal. Which reminds me that the last one to snooze off a gluttonous orgy on our post top last week was not as stuffed as most, and we have just realized that the pair of five-lined skinks that sunned and copulated on our shed stoop this spring have been missing since that time. We fear that they have by now been translated into the bones and supple sinew of one of their reptilian cousins.

But perpendicular climbing is not the only rouser in this snake's bag of tricks. On one occasion I entered the shed to discover a cast snakeskin four and one-half feet long draped from a nail point five feet above the floor and looped across various odds and ends, including the edge of a pane of window glass. As I examined it, I suddenly realized that I was looking at a negative, an everted retrograde, and that this was the backward, inside-out chronicle of events. This black rat snake had apparently been crawling along one of the two-by-four horizontal wall braces when it felt like taking off its skin and chose the protruding nail point on which to snag its lower lip. From there on it was just like pulling off a sock inside out.

The cast skin itself tells a good deal about its previous owner: whether its scales were keeled or not, the type of markings it had which are still faintly visible, and whether or not it was a pit viper. If the snake was one of the many varieties of harmless ones, then there will be just two nodes in the dried skin on the top of the head near the tip which indicate nostrils. If, however, there are four nodes, then the two nearest the eyes indicate the sensory organs of the pit viper. Four nodes on the skin's head combined with keeled scales are sufficient in this area to indicate the presence of a copperhead, and the faint, ghostly, hourglass pattern is usually visible enough to supply corroborative evidence.

My very first encounter with a black rat snake was something of a shock. I had unlimbered my fly rod one afternoon with the hope of coaxing some bluegills into my fish basket, and as I approached the water's edge in the grove at the shallow end of the pond, I was startled to see in a small, sunlit clearing a large, black snake with an immense greenish horn protruding from each side of its head. At first I was inclined to lay the blame for this herpetological nightmare on the quality and ingredients of my favorite liquid refreshment, but after batting my eyes several times, the mist cleared, and I realized that I had just caught a black rat snake at an awkward moment. It had just begun to ingest a sizable frog headfirst when I blundered onto the glade, its jaws were dislocated to accommodate the bulk being swallowed, and regurgitation was impossible. As for the hapless frog, he was already halfway down the tube, and his legs were sticking out rigidly, one from each side of the snake's mouth. Infinitely relieved that I had been spared delirium tremens, I left the snake to its own devices. When I passed the spot on my way back to the house sometime later, it was gone, presumably to a safe, lofty niche somewhere to snooze and restore its tissues.

Black rat snakes are something of a problem for us. They are powerful constrictors, are an immense help in controlling rodents in this area, and account in part for the fact that we are rarely troubled with rats and mice in the house. They also share the same diet with the copperheads and compete with them for the available food supply, thus thinning out the venomous snake population. But, unfortunately, they also have a taste for young bluebirds, thrashers, and other birds that prefer to nest within the limits of their climbing ability. On the whole, though, the balance is in their favor, and we allow them the run of the place.

The pond provides a home for only one species of snake as far as we know, and that is the common water snake, *Natrix sipedon*. He is plainly visible at times, zipping across the surface of the water at a good clip and leaving an ever expanding V in his wake. At other times he hugs the shoreline, fitting his body to every convolution of the bank as he moves slowly along in search of food. This is the fellow who tries from time to time to work his way into our wire-mesh fish basket, and woe betide the foolish fisherman who settles for a plain stringer for his catch if a couple of common water snakes are around. They will eat his fish dinner for him and hang around for more. One of these snakes, whom we dubbed Long John, frequently passed by our feet as we fished. I found his cast skin in the weeds one day, and it measured exactly four feet in length. We are sure he had an appetite to match his dimensions and would raise havoc with any bluegills or baby muskrats he could get hold of.

These snakes have more than their share of trouble. To the uninitiated, which includes most of the people who come to fish at our pond, any snake in the water is a cottonmouth water moccasin, and although the poor common water snake bears little resemblance to this dangerous species, the average fisherman will, on sight, grab the first thing to come to hand, be it a tree branch, a cane pole, an oar, or even a shotgun, and proceed to belt or blast away until he has reduced this harmless snake to a meringue. Despite the fact that there are absolutely no cottonmouths this far west of the coastal plain, this flannel-headed water flailer will then parade around with the pitiful remains dangling from a stick and go on authoritatively and at great length about the pugnacity of this species and the potency of its venom.

The bystanders, of course, swallow this story lox, shlock, and bagel, and if anyone has the gall to point out that it is not a cottonmouth at all, the spellbinder will stalk off in high dudgeon. Obviously, he finds that the dramatic fiction lies far more sweetly on his tongue than would the flat admission of simple fact, and being a fisherman, he loves to tell a good story, true or not.

Unfortunately, the "moccasin" business is quite a muddle, and it is not helped a bit by a well-known dictionary, which lumps all pit vipers of the genus *Agkistrodon*, particularly *A. piscivorus*, under that heading. This dictionary then goes on to identify the water moccasin not only as *A. piscivorus* but also as any harmless water snake that might be mistaken for it. As a result, everyone in the eastern half of the United States will swear up and down that there are water moccasins where he lives, and I am reduced to muttering "mokeson-moccasin" to myself and sticking straws in my hair.

But mokesons and moccasins aside, it is *A. contortrix,* our ubiquitous neighborhood copperhead, that poses a continual threat to our well-being in the warmer months. It is not that these snakes are constantly popping up all around us, but rather that they could be hidden almost anywhere but seldom are. There is where the danger lies, for we unconsciously develop a false sense of security after years of watchfulness, only to encounter one where we least expect it. Imagine picking one's way carefully for years around brushy sloughs, rotten logs, and rocky hillsides and avoiding unlighted parts of the lawn at night only to blunder headlong into a large one in the newly mown backyard in broad daylight. Imagine also wading knee-deep, spring after spring, through tangles of Virginia creeper, wild grape, honeysuckle, cow-itch vine, and poison ivy to reach the most luscious of the blackberries and never encountering any snakes at all, and then uncovering a copperhead with the lawn mower in a foot-square clump of grass beside the backyard mulch pile. This happened to be a small one, to be sure, but the female copperhead is a live bearer, and her young emerge into the world, like Athena from the head of Zeus, fully armed and ready for business, and their little hypodermic syringes are extremely efficient.

Copperhead bites are rarely fatal, but they can be extremely painful, and a well-placed bite on the ankle can make one's leg swell up like a cottage ham. We once had an acquaintance who was bitten on the middle finger of the right hand. Since, through a misunderstanding, medical attention was delayed, nerve damage resulted, and the individual lost all feeling in the finger and all use of it. For me, as a professional musician, something like this would be intolerable, so while we pursue a strict policy of *laissez faire* where harmless snakes are concerned, we dispatch without hesitation any copperhead who crosses our path. But even so, I don't like the odds. There's always another copperhead, and as was true of the water boy in the old song, I don't know where he's hiding.

## XII

# Big Turkle!

"YOU WANT TO HOLD OR CHOP?"
"I chop 'im."

I passed the axe to Willie and turned to the garbage can that served as a temporary holding pen for the snapper. The turtle was a big one, a twenty-five pounder, that Willie had hooked while fishing in our pond and managed to play until I came galumphing up with the dip net and heaved it ashore. I had hoped that he would take it off in the topless carton I offered, but he assured me, with wide-eyed solemnity, that he was not taking *that* to his bosom.

Since there was nothing else to carry it in alive, it was obvious that the beheading would have to take place on the premises and that I was to be master of ceremonies. The turtle was on its hind legs, leaning against the side of the can and glaring at me with baleful yellow eyes. Displeased with what it saw, it opened its powerful, toothless jaws and hissed. Clearly, it had the same Sam Smallish, I-hate-you-one-and-all-damn-your-eyes disposition that the rest of its species had. I eased the can over on its side, slid the turtle to the ground, and grasped it firmly by the tail. As I lifted it, the head snaked out, hoping for a whack at my brisket, but as soon as the front of the plastron touched the surface of the chopping block the head was quickly withdrawn and the waiting began. I maintained a firm grip on the tail, keeping the turtle's rear slightly elevated, until its head emerged again to take stock of the situation, extending further and further. Then the axe blade flashed with one clear, clean stroke from Willie, and the deed was done.

Willie went on his way rejoicing with visions of sweet, tender turtle fried in egg and cornmeal dancing in his head, but I did not envy him the hot, messy afternoon which lay ahead. He will need a cauldron of scalding water, a short, sharp knife with plenty of backbone, and a lot of elbow grease before this behemoth winds up in the pan.

A brief immersion in the hot water, using the tail as a handle, will suffice to soften the skin and claws so that they may be readily removed, but then the real work begins. The turtle will be placed on its back and steadied with blocks or wedges firmly affixed to the table surface to eliminate any rocking or sliding caused by the rounded carapace. The plastron will then be loosened by severing with the tip of the knife blade the cartilaginous material which binds the plastron to the carapace. With the plastron retained as a movable but still useful pressure point, the knife will then be inserted along the interior surface of the carapace to loosen the meat from the shell, particularly at the points where the heavy leg muscles are attached. With this accomplished, the plastron will then be removed, the viscera extracted, and the edible remainder cut into sizes suitable for frying. Also, since Willie's turtle is a big one, it will be necessary to make filets of the neck and leg meat, which will otherwise be too thick to fry properly.

Good luck to Willie and his turtle dressing. Meanwhile I have the severed head to deal with. There are many old wives' tales which have long since been discredited, but when those worthy crones advised not to pick up a newly severed snapper head, they were not just mumbling in their gruel. The things can bite. Hard. I found a stout twig and rapped the snout. Nothing. Another rap. No response. The third rap did it. The jaws had the twig in a death grip, and I tossed them both into a briar patch for the ultimate delectation of whatever was interested. I never cease to marvel, and as often as I've done it this recurring ritual never fails to bring to mind the time in my high school biology lab when a snapping turtle's heart lay beating hour after hour in a saline solution, while, in an adjacent bubbling beaker, the same turtle's flesh was being loosened from its skeleton. Such is the tenacious grip these creatures have on life.

Turtles are plentiful in and around Two-Moon Pond: mud turtles, box turtles, cooters, pond sliders, the smelly little stinkpots, and the spotted turtles that my Ocracoke friends call "highland hicketies." But by far the most plentiful are those tough, formidable holdovers from the Pleistocene like the one Willie and I had just dispatched.

# Big Turkle!

*Chelydra serpentina* is a pretty fancy name for a grim old U-boat of a beast that spends its winters in some muddy burrow and the warmer seasons lying in wait on the pond bottom or cruising below the surface seeking anything those merciless jaws can crunch. But having little Latin and less Greek, it remains unperturbed by polysyllabic niceties and continues its ceaseless predatory rounds.

This year, after a particularly severe winter, I saw a snapper's conning tower rise for the first time on a blustery first of March. It apparently liked what it saw, and with plenty of food available, it appeared more and more frequently as the weather warmed, and it was soon joined by others.

The snapper's tastes are catholic, to say the least. Newts, fish, crayfish, snakes, muskrats, smaller members of its own species—anything, in short, that lives and moves in the pond of a size worth the trouble is considered fair game. Fishermen must look sharp to their stringers, particularly if any fish they catch are bleeding, and waterfowl are in great danger of being seized from below, never to rise again. This spring, for example, a female red-breasted merganser disappeared below the surface with flaps of protest before our eyes. When we reached the spot, a subaqueous old meat-grinder of a snapping turtle was already tearing it to shreds. But despite the fabled voracity of these turtles, their depredations have had only a minor impact on our pond life. We keep no domestic waterfowl, and I feel certain that they are no more of a threat to the fish population than the kingfishers, herons, and ospreys who are regular visitors. And since they are a definite asset where muskrat control is concerned, I bid them Godspeed, and, unless they are inadvertently hooked by Willie, allow them to cruise unvexed.

With the coming of April and the warming of the

water, the snappers are moved to participate in what passes with them for the process of reproduction. The encounter usually takes place in the northeast quadrant of the pond and always on the surface. A thrashing tumult in the water is the signal that an amatory engagement is under way, and year after year I play the voyeur, fascinated by what seems to be one of the most brutal copulative procedures in nature.

It is clear at the outset that neither of the pair can stand the sight of the other. The male is the aggressor who will not be denied, while the female is equally determined that she will see him sliced to ribbons before she will submit. And so they face off like two Civil War rams, maneuvering slowly for an advantage, edging into striking position so that their sharp, hooked beaks can be brought into play. After forty-five minutes or an hour of this cut-and-slash, the raw, pink flesh of their gashed heads and necks is plainly visible, and it is only then that the male finds the opportunity he seeks. Although he initially mounts from the rear, a flattish plastron fits poorly on a rounded cara-pace, and soon they are plastron to plastron, locked in a love-hate embrace which sets them slowly barrel-rolling until their union is consummated. The rolling procedure is quite necessary, as it turns out, since, because of the overhang of the carapace and the leeway afforded by the plastron, only the bottom turtle, upside down, can get its head out of the water to breathe.

When at last they part, the impregnated female swims slowly off to the shallow, muddy end of the pond while the male, his stint in the lists of love complete, lies puffing and wheezing on the surface until he gets his wind back and can resume his interminable search for something else to snap at.

A Hindu mystic was once asked about his concept of

the earth, and he replied that the earth was an island floating on water in a huge bowl resting on the back of an enormous elephant, which was supported by a colossal turtle. When asked what held the turtle up, he indicated that it rested on yet another even greater turtle. When pressed further he finally replied, "Let's face it: there's always another turtle." And so it is at Two-Moon Pond. Catch them as we will, there is a seemingly endless supply of snappers, for there are ten ponds of an acre or more within a half-mile of ours, and when the wanderlust is on them, they may well leave the old homestead and move off to more congenial waters. On a number of occasions, by day or night, I have come upon them, lumbering across the lawn like miniature Sherman tanks and headed for my pond. One moonlit night, in fact, I went to investigate a hitherto unnoticed hump in the lawn and found myself standing near the water's edge in the immediate rear of a large snapper. As I bent over for a closer look, it suddenly wheeled 180 degrees with remarkable agility for a creature so cumbersome and made for the protection of the water. I was in the way, of course, but not for long. I bounded into the air like a springbok, and when I landed, the turtle had vanished into the dark pond. From that time forth, I did my nighttime hummock checking from a respectful distance with a flashlight.

Perhaps the greatest problem in playing host to these big, surly brutes is that occasionally one will swim too close to the vertical run-off pipe during overflow and find itself firmly pasted in place by suction. The protective shield around the mouth of the pipe has long since turned to ferrous oxide, and only a stub of the cedar post which once supported it remains above water. As a result, whenever a snapper gets hung up it must be removed, either manually from a boat or by trying to snag a flange of its shell with a large Hopkins lure and a surf rod from the shore. Manual removal from a boat is not bad if the turtle is in headfirst and half strangled, but if it has made contact plastron down, it is usually in a towering rage and firmly stuck. To get it free without benefit of a stable platform and adequate leverage is dangerous and almost impossible. I therefore prefer to cast twenty feet with the treble-hooked lure until a purchase is secured and heave. The turtle usually comes loose with a mighty slurp, and the overflow continues. As for the Hopkins lure, that always winds up somewhere in the big winged elm immediately behind me. I lose a lot of Hopkins lures that way.

And so the wheeling seasons come and go, and in and around our little watery world the snappers lurk in some secluded hideaways or slip effortlessly like gray-green shadows through the dark water, pausing now and then to up snorkel without a ripple and as quietly disappear. But inevitably, the day will come when there will be a cry of "Big turkle!" from Willie, and it's the dip net detail once again for me.

XIII

# *What Gets under My Skin*

As NORTHERN TRANSPLANTS IN THE RURAL NORTH Carolina Piedmont, my wife and I have taken root readily enough and have adapted ourselves to the minor differences in climate, fauna, and flora. The springs come a little earlier than those we knew, and the clear, bright, seemingly endless golden southern autumns fade almost imperceptibly until, at long last, in November, a boreal wind strips the remaining leaves from the trees and sends them skittering helter-skelter across the lawn and drive.

The mixed stands of pine, eastern red cedar, and holly

which hold the green line against winter were also new to us, of course, as were the interminable roulades of the mockingbird and the sinuous menace of the copperhead, but on the whole we were still living within the bounds of the great central hardwood forest, substantially the same natural environment we had experienced in our youth.

But there is one notable exception: insects—pestiferous insects which, together with certain arthropods, lust after our flesh and blood or seem to feel that our aspects and general conditions would be vastly improved if our skins had more holes in them.

In the North we had an occasional mosquito, bee, or wasp. Now and then a housefly would choose one's nose as a promenade, and who indeed has not met the ubiquitous cockroach? But here dwell six- and eight-legged creatures of such infinite variety, strange appetites, and fiendish ingenuity as to make one think that Nature, having outdone herself in creating a green and pleasant land, decided to inject a little torment into the natives' lives to ginger them up a bit and keep them from adopting shiftless and sloppy ways.

Take chiggers or redbugs, for instance. In their minute six-legged larval stage they lurk in tall grass and vegetation until a human host brushes by. They attach themselves to the clothing, head for the skin, and then, in utter denial of all decorum, seek out the softest, moistest, most constricted portions of the anatomy, burrow in, and set up housekeeping. The result of this incursion is red welts and an infernal itching in delicate and inaccessible places which is enough to curdle the creamiest disposition. An effective insect repellant broadly applied to one's entire body is the only safeguard against such gross transgressions, unless one happens to have natural immunity.

*What Gets under My Skin*

Such a repellant can also make one proof against the dog tick, which is the vector for Rocky Mountain spotted fever. With two cases of this debilitating and sometimes fatal disease reported in our immediate neighborhood, we take the matter very seriously indeed in warm weather. My wife, in fact, considers herself a tick magnet and, unprotected, cannot walk to a nearby clothesline and back without finding old *Dermacentor venustus* creeping around her collar or up her skirt.

As for the wasps in our area, we have developed a rule of thumb to determine their aggressiveness. If they are drab brown or black, they are usually one or another of the mud daubers or paper wasps, which are peaceable, hard-working, live-and-let-live insects, some of which are extremely beneficial. I have seen a swarm of wasps totally eradicate a caterpillar infestation on an oak tree branch by the simple expedient of slicing them, like so many salamis, into transportable sections and flying off with them. Another species has an interest in cabbage loopers, which they decapitate and squeeze with their mandibles like tubes of toothpaste. The juicy, green, extruded innards are then rolled into neat English pea–sized balls and hauled off for the delectation of their young. But even a mud dauber will brook no interference, as my wife discovered when, doused with repellant, she inadvertently got between one and its nest. Without a moment's hesitation it drew its claymore and pinked her neatly in the upper arm.

Even those big flying cigar butts, the cicada-killers, will live among humans without incident. A number of these solitary wasps have dwelt in the ground under a clump of bushes on a busy corner of a university campus for at least twenty-five years and have even entered classrooms through unscreened windows, with consequences

83

no more dire than momentary anxiety and distraction among some students whose attention spans were not remarkable in the first place.

If a wasp's predominant coloration is yellow, though, then that is another bag of beans entirely. The various species of so-called yellow jackets seem to be ill-tempered, vindictive, and constantly on the prod. A swarm of these fiends built a nest quite out of sight under our rural mailbox and incised periods, commas, and semicolons in my hide every time I came near. I had almost run out of exclamation points before I located the nest and fogged them out from upwind.

But they were cooing turtledoves compared with those savage yellow devils that live in the ground near the south gate by the pond. My mere presence is enough to send one of these hellions into a screaming fury, and it will then undertake to drive me not just away but all the way back to the house and out of its sight. The first time I was attacked by one I laid down my fishing rod and beat a harassed retreat toward the house. After a hundred feet of this nonsense, I no longer heard it and turned back. At that instant it stuck its little spontoon in just under my right eye and, with a contemptuous waggle of wings, flew back to rejoin its escadrille. Now, when one of those supercharged demons goes whining past my ear, this is one little dogie that really "gits along" to the screened front porch. Or even to Wyoming, if necessary.

"Watch out for hornets," I was told when I first set out berrying, but I found this to be an inaccurate injunction. You can't watch out for hornets; there's nothing to see. Flies buzz, bees hum, and beetles drone, but when I hear something that sounds like a band saw going through a green pine knot, a steady, angry snarl rich in upper partials, I know that I have roused a bald-faced hornet and am being given fair warning. If I back off a bit, I'll be let alone, but if I proceed, it will go home and sound the tocsin. Then its cohorts will come zapping out of the hole at the bottom of that big paper coconut of a nest like rounds from a Gatling gun. Not wishing a severely perforated integument, I sidle meekly off and do my berrying elsewhere.

Actually, bald-faced hornets away from their nests are quite easy to get along with. They have always tolerated my passage as they scrape wood fibers off my pasture gate for nest-building material, and when I am painting with latex paint, I have often had them land on my hand or arm to investigate the daubs and dribbles with which I am usually generously endowed. Not wanting to stir up a fuss, I allow them to remain until their curiosity is satisfied, and not one of them has slipped its shiv into me yet.

One insect that really bugged me, though, was Old Blood-and-Guts, a big, aggressive, black bee that holed up somewhere behind the battens of the lean-to near my fish-cleaning table one summer. For some reason, it loved to muck about in the blood and slime of eviscerated fish and frequently came snoring around my hapless head when I was cleaning them. I, of course, would back off, whereupon the black bruiser would take over the table with its spread of offal, and the fish dinner would have to wait unless I was able to sneak up on hands and knees and make off with what I could grab. I have done some curious things in my time, but I never thought the day would come when I'd be stealing my own fish back from a bee.

A real danger is lurking in some dark crannies and hidey-holes on our premises. The black widow spider, that swart, secret spinner, thrives in obscurity and responds to bodily contact with an extremely venomous and sometimes deadly bite. Inverted cans and flower pots, boots, gauntlets, woodpiles, the hollows of cement building blocks, the undersides of privy seats, and even the undersides of watermelons, all suit the black widows as residences.

In view of their great adaptability to bizarre habitats and the fact that I do not as yet aspire to realms celestial, I am very careful where I insert my hands and feet and give my stored firewood a thorough thumping before bringing it into the house. The sight of *Latrodectus mactans* emerging stiff-legged from a hollow log on a chilly night and executing in the warm firelight a somber sarabande on my hearthstone is something I can do without. Were there others I hadn't seen?

While most of the insects and arthropods who delight in violating my dermal integrity are specialists in acupuncture and/or hypodermic injections, there is one creature who, like Shylock, claims its due in the form of red meat. We had our first encounter in my butter-bean patch when I heard a crackle of wings and felt a series of scratchy sensations and a twinge of pain on my forearm. At first glance I thought I had been assaulted by a large katydid, but when I noticed that its mandibles were buried in my flesh and its mouth parts were busily chewing away I knew that this was not just a happy-go-lucky stridulator and it was not fiddling around; it was trying to eat. Me!

I managed to get it disengaged and examined it closely. It was green, more than an inch and a half long, with a saber-shaped ovipositor of almost equal length, a pointed head, and those powerful mandibles which, when they were extracted, left two tiny drops of blood on my skin three thirty-seconds of an inch apart. This was a female *Neoconocephalus*, the cone-headed grasshopper, and if its voracious behavior toward me was indicative, a formidable predator. After addressing it with a few short, well-chosen words in bald Anglo-Saxon, I released it in the hope that it might give my bean beetles pause.

In view of the extreme bugginess of the rest of the property, we fully expected that the acre pond in our front yard would be a breeding spot for clouds of mosquitoes, that the swale at dusk would be loud with anticipatory humming, and that we would ultimately be reduced to puffy, itching travesties of our former selves. As luck would have it, we had friends and allies on our side—fish, frogs, toads, newts, dragonflies, swallows, swifts, martins, fly-catchers, nighthawks, and bats—and thus far we have been spared. For this mercy we are indeed truly grateful. Enough is enough.

# XIV

# *Rubus, Rubus, I've Been Thinking*

EACH JULY I BLEED A LITTLE. BY THEN, THE PINK blossoms which graced the interlocking arches of the thick, coarse, red-streaked green canes along the back fence have been replaced by pendulous panicles of huge globular blackberries, and it's time once again to belly up to the thorny wall of briars and harvest what is within reach.

This is not one of the two hundred and five or more species of *Rubus fruticosis* whose white blossoms spangle the ditches and hedgerows across much of central and eastern North America at about the time that the bluegills fan out their saucer-shaped nests in the pond shallows in springtime. Secretive by nature, this variety scorns such flamboyant display and prefers to snake a long, sinuous course through the meadow grass, where its blossoms and fruit are almost invisible to the passerby.

In spite of their shy and withdrawn disposition, though, these canes managed to bring themselves to my attention when I tripped over a hidden one and was sent sprawling with a cruelly lacerated instep. Muttering sulphurous curses against such covert villainy, I lopped off the offending "weed" and consigned it and its kind to the outer limits of perdition. It wasn't until I found several canes that had been spared during spring haying and tasted their splendid fruit that I realized that under controlled conditions this would not be a weed at all but a fruit well worth cultivation.

As chance would have it, I was in the process of rooting out a formidable hedgerow of *Rosa multiflora* and discovered, woven in the incredible tangle, the very type of canes which had been a snare unto my feet. Painstakingly I unraveled and removed the offending rambler to give the berry canes a fighting chance, and the following spring I was rewarded with a twenty-foot spread of large, pink blossoms, which, in July, provided me with gallon after gallon of lustrous black globes of six-to-the-handful size.

But maintaining "controlled conditions" has proved to be a continuous and maddening task. The soil here is fertile, the rainfall adequate, and the vegetation lush. As the heavy canes arch over the barbed-wire fence, they are soon infiltrated by the ineradicable and indefatigable *Rosa multiflora* as well as by fox grape, honeysuckle, poison ivy, black walnut and honey locust seedlings, and a wide variety of annual weeds. Since there is absolutely no way of eradicating the rampant undergrowth without destroying the valuable roots and canes, I make a point of cleaning out the unwanted growth every winter when, thank God, things stop growing for a little while. Then in the spring, I make a daily patrol of the patch and snip off any undesirable shoot that sticks its head into full sunlight. This gives the berry canes, blossoms, and fruit a badly needed edge in the struggle for survival and puts a check on the riotous enthusiasm of the intruders.

I must admit that picking berries in this mess is something of an ordeal. Unlike the young rabbit that finds shelter and security in this thicket, I am a gross and clumsy alien, thin-skinned and often greedily incautious. For me to enter this lacerating tangle, then, is to venture into an environment of implacable hostility and remorseless rigor where every error in judgment is atoned for immediately with blood and pain.

At first I took up the task fully clothed, even to the point of wearing gloves, only to find that many of the juiciest clusters lay just behind a lattice of intersecting canes. The gloves snagged, my clothing snagged, I dropped berries, and a sudden movement placed under tension and then released a stout cane which had slyly attached itself to my shirtsleeve. The resultant whiplash left me with a shredded ear, a bloody shirt, and a vitriolic disposition.

I now do my picking in sandals, shorts, a T-shirt, and a hat. I move slowly and gently, calculating every step and avoiding, if possible, any motion perpendicular to the axes of those incredible thorns with their stiletto tips. I must keep in mind that any portion of my anatomy which enters that *chevaux-de-frise* must come out by that same door wherein it went. I have become a study in slow motion and never, never forget what lies immediately behind me, particularly if it is the bucket with the morning's pickings in it. Oh, the thorns still draw a little claret now and then, but I no longer show up for lunch looking as though I had just been embraced by the Iron Maiden of Nuremberg.

From the first I was curious about the identity of this formidable but productive species and questioned some local old-timers. They shrugged and shook their heads. I got in touch with the county agent, who came, beheld, marveled, but knew it not. Next I called the botany departments of several universities in the area, and they provided me with the following information:

a. They had never heard of it.
b. Since they had never heard of it, it probably didn't exist.
c. If it did in fact exist, it was unimportant.
d. No! They did not wish to see it.

Frustrated by the experienced, the professional, and the learned, I suddenly remembered my copy of Everard and Morley's exquisitely illustrated *Wildflowers of the World*. There it was on plate nine, beautifully limned in every detail, *Rubus ulmifolius*, the elm-leaved blackberry of west, south, and central Europe, northwestern Africa, and the Canary Islands.

So I'm playing host to an immigrant, then, but from whence it came exactly, and when, and under whose sponsorship I shall never know. But here at least is one imported species which, unlike Japanese honeysuckle, Japanese beetles, starlings, weaver finches, and kudzu, has managed to make a great deal more than an unconscionable nuisance of itself.

## XV

# This Reviving Herb

IT WAS ALL WELL AND GOOD FOR OMAR KHAYYAM TO
sing sweetly of the tender green that fledged the river
lip he leaned on, but five will get you fifty that he had
neither lawn to mow nor garden to weed. If he had, then
Fitzgerald would likely have come across a rubaiya which
read:

> Long hours have I pushed this damned machine
> To mow down swaths of tall, relentless green;
> Yet on the morrow must I root more out
> From carrot, cauliflower, pea, and bean.

Old Omar had it nice. No spacious greensward of Bermuda grass, crabgrass, Johnson grass, fescue, plantain, dandelion, and wild garlic to run riot the minute his back was turned. But if I do, it's no one's fault but my own. When we first moved to Two-Moon Pond, the pasture fence ran six feet from the bedroom end of the house, and the mooing and chomping of livestock just outside our window at daybreak was not conducive to repose. I was determined to put the cows in their place, but my snap decisions resulted in a typical instance of overkill, for when the fences were moved to my specifications, the landscaping completed, and the grass growing, I found myself staring in horror at the better part of an acre of new lawn.

The nine hundred square feet set aside for the vegetable garden scarcely put a dent in the amount of mowing required, and the garden itself, of course, proved vulnerable to infestation by the usual weeds. Most of them proved easy enough to control, but two species adamantly refuse to this day to knuckle under to my governance. They wage a kind of guerrilla warfare which involves uprisings in unexpected places at inconvenient times. The severest of my pogroms serve only to drive them to the fringes of the contested area and to the shelter of mulch and low, wide-spreading plants. There they bide their time and muster their forces until conditions are favorable to launch another assault against my innocent vegetables in the hope of driving them and me away for good. More and more I find myself playing Pershing to their Pancho Villa.

One of the ringleaders in this green revolution is the henbit, *Lamium amplexicaule*. This pretentious pest is an alien of the mint family and suffers from delusions of grandeur. It fancies itself as a wildflower and is in fact so listed in the field guides and handbooks, but you won't catch me weaving it into any garlands gay.

It's not that the henbit with its opposite, rounded, scalloped leaves and small, delicate, pinkish-purple flowers is unattractive, for it has a certain rustic charm and grace. Unfortunately, it is maniacally reproductive, pushy, and intrusive, and in the process, it commits the unforgivable sin of being common. Unquestionably our perception of a species' beauty varies inversely to its prevalence. If the henbit were to become an endangered species, for instance, and as rare as the showy lady's slipper, we would soon find ourselves prating about its dainty form and exquisite color and would turn heaven and earth to preserve it for future generations. Conversely, if the showy lady's slipper were suddenly to run as rife in our vegetable gardens as henbit, we would soon be deploring its garishness and ubiquity and destroying it on sight. But there is little danger that the henbit will become extinct. Rosemary may be for remembrance, but henbit is forever.

Vexatious as this weed may be, however, the palm for causing severe pangs in my *glutei* must go to that unspeakable excrescence, Bermuda grass. Let those who will sing of its excellence as a lawn or pasture grass; to me it is anathema. In keeping with its sneaky character, it travels under various aliases—wire grass, scutch grass, dog's tooth grass, Bahama grass, and devil's grass—and the last is the most apt. Whatever hell is paved with, you may be certain that Bermuda grass is growing in the cracks.

Mulch, they tell me, will inhibit weeds, and as far as the feebler, faint-hearted varieties are concerned, this is true. But lusty Bermuda grass, firmly established in the fescue at the garden's edge, will simply smirk and insolently send its stolons over it in no time. Cut these shoots and it will send more, this time *under* the mulch. Cut these, and it will burrow like so many earthworms as deep as a foot underground, constantly poking up tentative, delicate shoots which totally belie the wiry, robust tangle of runners lurking underneath the soil. The invasion has begun, and if it is not caught in time, a permanent bed of raspberries or asparagus is doomed, for this grass can never be rooted out without damaging the established plants.

The subterranean stolons can also knit themselves into a tight ball as big as one's head, which will set a five-horsepower tiller humping and bucking like a bronco in a futile effort to chew through. And there is no point in chopping it up to destroy it. Like a sliced-up starfish, every segment is capable of generating a new entity. Devil's grass indeed! May the devil take it!

In isolated nooks and crannies, around woodpiles, in the rough, rocky patches at the margins of the meadow, along the fences, and among the permanent plantings of shrubs and bushes around the house are insurgents of a different kind, mainly woody vines and seedling trees. Their location is determined by the presence of their seeds in the droppings of perching birds. It is claimed by some that a seed's viability is often enhanced by a trip through a bird's alimentary canal. However that may be, I can certainly attest to the fact that such a passage seems to do the seeds little harm, judging by the profusion and vigor of these squatters, some of which are not really weeds at all but, rather, desirable species in poor locations from a gardener's point of view.

And so our foundation plantings of azalea, Chinese holly, camellia, elaeagnus, japonica, and nandina serve inadvertently as a kind of nursery not only for blackberry canes, poison ivy, pokeweed, wild clematis, and fox grape, but for a wide variety of trees—wild black cherry, holly, hackberry, dogwood, eastern red cedar, sassafras, mimosa, redbud, mulberry, and honey locust—all of which, thanks to our little feathered distributors, are situated near the bases of the shrubs and go largely unnoticed until they burst triumphantly through the bushes' crowns. My annoyance at having to root them out is moderated somewhat, though, by the fact that we have a constant supply of dogwood, American holly, and redbud seedlings to transplant as needed.

Another tree-distributing agent is the gray squirrel. Thievish, persistent, and engagingly insolent, it robs me of all the black walnuts it can get its paws on and buries them, as well as hickory nuts and acorns, in every place imaginable. Unfortunately, the squirrels seem to subscribe to the notion that the sooner you bury something, the sooner you can forget about it. This often leaves me with some undetected hardwood seedlings whose deep taproots cannot be removed without disturbing established shrubs and have such amazing regenerative capacity that new shoots will be propagated year after year despite repeated cutbacks.

A marked change in a microenvironment may even produce an unexpected surge of growth which, unchecked, could prove devastating. There is a narrow stretch between the back of the shed and the fence which was at one time sheltered by a huge spreading hackberry tree. This was the place where, protected from the wind, dappled by morning sunlight, and shaded from the westering sun, my potted tuberous begonias grew best. Weeds grew poorly or not at all here, and access was uninhibited.

One winter brought a severe ice storm, though, and under the weight of hundreds of pounds of glaze the great tree suddenly groaned like a taxpayer in April as its massive trunk tore apart. Split from top to bottom, it was clearly done for. No more birds would shelter in its branches or seek out its berries, and the orchard orioles would have to sling their hammock of a nest elsewhere. Regretfully, I had it removed.

It was at this time that my wife got into an acrimonious tussle with a rosebush and sustained a back injury which laid her up for more than a year. The responsibilities for cooking, shopping, laundry, and the maintenance of the household fell into my less-than-competent hands, and I discharged them in such a way that by the time my wife was on her feet again, I had been dubiously honored by receiving the *Poor Housekeeping* Sloven-of-the-Year award, first class, with dustball cluster.

During my tenure as *homo domesticus*, then, my outside activities were limited to my job and what was minimally necessary to keep the vegetable garden going. Consequently, two summers had passed before I ventured behind the shed again, where I was stopped cold by eight-foot pokeweeds, countless hackberry seedlings, rampaging honeysuckle, and well-sinewed cow-itch vines. They all now had a place in the sun and were going hell-for-leather.

As I hacked my way through this mini–rain forest, I discovered that the cow-itch vines had rack and ruin in their hearts and had insinuated themselves, wherever possible, between the shed's battens and siding, where they had expanded, forcing the battens away from the wall and exposing the apertures to the weather. Some vines had already inserted their tender tips between the underside of the roof and the siding. Clearly, in ten years' time with such growth unchecked, the shed would have been a wreck, and nature, with her sly, insinuating tentacles, would have reestablished suzerainty over a long-disputed territory.

And so the endless, seesaw struggle continues. Throughout each growing season I mow, hack, snip, and shlepp and line up the haymakers to mow and bale the green tide of meadow grass which twice each summer surges against the pasture fence. Autumn and winter bring a temporary cessation of hostilities, but with the February thaw the first hairy tufts of wild garlic show in the lawn and I know that, far to the south, the hosts of spring have flung their green gonfalons to the breeze and are marching implacably upon us.

.

## XVI

# *Under the Weather*

ONE WOULD HAVE TO BE AN UTTER TROGLODYTE TO deny that nothing in nature has a greater and more constant impact on our daily lives than the weather. Whether its effects are grossly obvious or subtly subliminal, it is woven into the fabric of our existence, and, awake or asleep, we respond to it in one way or another as the interaction of temperature, humidity, and barometric pressure causes changes in our individual plans, actions, moods, needs, and health, to say nothing of our collective economy and general welfare.

Most of us, at one time or another, have felt ourselves going emotionally rancid after being cooped up for days on end during foul winter weather or have had our nerve ends frazzle in an August heat blitz that would have made Shadrach blanch. And then there is the tight knot that forms in one's stomach when the National Weather Service announces a tornado watch and the wind begins to howl, or the sensation one gets, having taken shelter in a tin-roofed shed during a hailstorm, of being a beetle in a snare drum during a pep rally. But these fears and discomforts are paltry things compared with the crushing blow of having one's sole cash crop seared to a crisp, pounded to mush, or lashed to tatters before one's eyes, or worse yet, finding oneself homeless or bereaved.

I recall one infamous year when May, although affording us a modicum of moisture, managed to straddle spring by having one foot in February and the other in August, with the thermometer running itself ragged trying to keep up. But there was nothing indecisive about June. It turned off the water and lit the gas, and soon we were sizzling like burgers on a grill. The flower and vegetable gardens were sustained by such amounts of water as I could apply, but every well has a bottom, and after a year of severe drought and a declining water table, I had to water sparingly and hope that the pump didn't start sucking sand.

The lima beans were particularly hard hit by the heat, which deactivates the pollen, I'm told. As a result, while the vines were sturdy and bloomed profusely, very few pods formed. The elm-leaved blackberries, on the other hand, some under semi-cultivation and the rest scattered along the hedgerows, begin to bear in July and, while impervious to heat, must have moisture to fill out the fruit. Providing water for them, though, was out of the question, and one could only hope that Aquarius would get his act together and dump a bucket or two on us before it was too late.

How dry was it? The pond told the story. With more than a foot of the standpipe showing and bare earthen banks exposed, the pond was at least one-fifth short of its 1,630,000-gallon capacity. Such a drawdown was something of a mixed blessing. On the credit side was the withering of some marginal growth, the roots of which no longer had access to moisture, and the bunching up of fish in a reduced volume of water, which brought predators and prey into closer proximity. The debit side was more heavily weighted. The muskrats became disturbed by the exposure of their burrow entrances, which were clearly visible in the bare banks. In consequence, they dug new ones and so made further inroads into the stability of the shoreline. May the pox smite them! Either that or the hulking snapper I spotted lying offshore just opposite a new burrow entrance—a one-turtle blockade. I wished it good hunting.

Fortunately, the weather has more in its budget than megrims, misery, whey-faced terror, and sudden death, for if it can hurt it can also heal, and if it depresses it also rejuvenates, and what it withholds often lends savor to its beneficences. There is an immense exhilaration to be felt, for instance, after a long dry spell, as I sit on the sheltered back stoop and watch the dark, towering, rain-gravid clouds build in the southwest, coalesce, and then move almost imperceptibly toward me. The sky darkens, a hush falls on the land, and in the silence I hear at last the faint susurrus of distant falling rain, which builds steadily to a roar as a screen of liquid silver sweeps down the meadow and over the house and pond. And at such times, despite my age, I am moved to respond to an old song's suggestion by removing my epidermis and dancing around in my bones.

But this is the exception. What usually happens is that, in the late afternoon, similar clouds form, full-bosomed and *saftig*, in the southwest, their skirts fringed with rain, and sidle coyly in our direction. This builds high hopes for some relief for the dry and dusty garden, but as we are about to let the loud hosannahs ring, the frivolous twits lift the hems of their farthingales and go flouncing off, either northward to the west of us or eastward to the south. Having received about as much moisture as one would get from a couple of shakes of an aspergillum, we turn again, sorely graveled, to our hoses and buckets and hope for a better day.

"He that observeth the wind shall not sow; and he that regardeth the clouds shall not reap," says Ecclesiastes, as, presumably, he promotes the notion that there is no way of knowing what will happen next meteorologically and you might as well go ahead and take your chances. Modern technology, however, has raised meteorology to something approaching a science, and it now offers somewhat better data than one's eyes, an elevated wet finger, or the pangs in one's sacroiliac can provide. Besides, the variety and complexities of modern life make it imperative for many to have some idea what is likely to happen. To farmers, seamen, airline pilots, truckers, foresters, gardeners, fishermen, athletes, and all who spend a large portion of their working or recreational hours out-of-doors or in vehicles or ships subject to the vagaries of the elements, the weather is a factor to be observed and reckoned with. To ignore it may be to find oneself unnecessarily drenched, flooded, frozen, fried, struck by lightning, short of water, sucked up and blown into the next county, or otherwise abused.

There are always those, however, who ignore the wind and the clouds as well as their newspapers, radios, and televisions and inevitably wind up bobbing in the sauce. They are iced up on highways, washed down arroyos, electrocuted in hayfields, capsized in lakes, and lost in blizzards. Some of these innocents fish at Two-Moon Pond, and I never cease to marvel as they unlimber their tackle under a lowering sky and begin fishing in the teeth of an ominous, straight-edged squall line that is bearing down on them from the northwest. Fifteen minutes later, soaked to the skin and buffeted by winds strong enough to blow them bald-headed, they run squawking to the shelter of their car, firmly convinced that their traumata were the result of an elemental caprice directed at them personally. "But it was so nice when we left home," they bleat plaintively. "Who would have thought . . . ?"

For my part, with things to mow and things to grow and that often-patched spot on the lean-to roof that shouldn't leak but usually does, I pay close attention to weather reports and keep tabs on local wind direction and velocity, temperature, and rainfall. One of my first acts on arising, in fact, is to draw the curtain on the big window which faces north to the pond, the meadow across the pond, and the forest beyond. Here is the set for act one, scene one, of the daily drama.

Where wind and precipitation are concerned, the pond surface tells it all. In the bright sunshine of a breathless morning it may lie like a sheet of unflawed glass reflecting perfectly the sky and the immediate environs. If the wind stands northwest, the surface will be broken into serried ranks of wavelets or even whitecaps, depending on wind velocity, and all the flotsam will soon be neatly swept by this magic broom into the southeast corner, where it may easily be raked out. Under the caress of a southwest breeze

the pond will bear gentle ripples, and for reasons un-
known—unless falling barometric pressure is a factor—
the fishing should be good.

The wind from the eastern quadrant, though, is usually
a puffing, feverish, fitful thing which, under a gray sky,
gives the pond an oily, viscous appearance marred only by
occasional brief cat's-paws of ripples. At such times there
is dirty weather brewing, and a falling barometer not-
withstanding, the fishing will be abysmal.

Under precipitation the water may be dimpled by a
drizzle, boiling in a downpour, or shattered into seemingly jagged fragments by a pounding hailstorm. Only
the cold hand of winter can quiet this aqueous tattletale,
locking it in ice from bank to bank, except where a transient mallard or a diligent muskrat may have succeeded
in paddling a patch of open water.

And so, as the earth spins, the seasons come and go,
and the winds of heaven blow, we learn to live with our
climate, knowing that it is a temperate one and that for
each excess there will be, ultimately, a compensation. June
of that year was indeed searing and hardtack dry, but on
the first morning of July I awoke to the drumming of
mammy-daddies and flamadiddles in the downspout. Rain!
I drew the curtain and glanced at the pond. It was pour-
ing. A tropical depression had formed off the coast, and
we were receiving some of the benefits. Millions of little
osmotic pumps immediately began to force the stuff of
life through every trunk, stalk, and stolon, and garden,
field, and forest were aroused from their dusty torpor.

Relief at last! July, according to my rain gauge, brought
us a whopping 9.69 inches, putting the pond's water level
over the top of the greedily sucking standpipe. Once again,
the healing had begun.

# XVII

# The Old Road

IF G. K. CHESTERTON HAD IT RIGHT, IT WAS THE rolling English drunkard who made the rolling English road, and if the old, original portion of Cornwallis Road we came to live on was not strictly English, geographically speaking, it met all the other requirements for it was laid out by an Englishman, and as previously noted, roll it most definitely did.

As for its maker, it was not General Cornwallis, as many suppose, but rather William Tryon, the British colonial governor of North Carolina from 1765 to 1771. Whether he was a rolling drunkard or not cannot be definitively stated, but certainly he was a Briton of his time with sufficient means to afford as much port, hock, sherry, and brandywine as was needed to offset boredom and the lack of central heating.

If he did in fact have a glass too much on occasion, he doubtless had his reasons. After all, there he was, off in the boondocks of colonial America, far from the London fleshpots, trying to keep the King's peace from being violated by, in his opinion, as scurvy a pack of rebellious rascals as one shall see in a summer's day.

They called themselves Regulators, and they lived mainly in the western part of the colony. In rebellion against oppressive government policies and practices, they committed acts of violence against government officials and property in Hillsborough, and in early 1771 Governor Tryon raised almost one thousand militia at forty shillings a head to move against them.

He found, however, that there was only a bridle path connecting Raleigh, where the existing road ended, with Hillsborough and so ordered a road to be made to accommodate the troops and wagons. This was done, and he named it the Ramsgate Road.

Tryon and his troops finally reached Hillsborough in the spring of 1771 and pressed on to Alamance Creek. There they confronted and defeated two thousand undisciplined and roistering Regulators on May 10 and took fifteen prisoners. One was summarily shot by way of intimidation, and the remaining fourteen were marched to Hillsborough and tried. Six were found guilty, and the court, contrary to modern practice, decided that, rather than suspend the sentence, they would suspend the Regulators. In Hillsborough, in the June of 1771, the six were duly hanged.

And so, out of upheaval and bloodshed, the rolling Ramsgate Road was born and proved a boon to the farmers and landowners of the area. But in addition to the obvious benefits they bring, roads also have a tendency to draw traffic and trouble as horse droppings draw flies. Such was the case when, in February of 1781, after the Battle of Cowpens and a fruitless pursuit of General Greene's army to the Dan River, General Cornwallis and his badly mauled and ill-provisioned troops fell back on their primary supply base at Hillsborough. Here it was discovered that the provisions promised by the loyalists (who were predominant in the area) had not been delivered, and the cupboard was bare. As a result, foraging parties were sent out, and there is no doubt that the Ramsgate Road provided them with easy access to such supplies as were available. It is no wonder that the Tory farmers cursed as they saw their oxen and even their draft horses being led off to the regimental cookpots and their goods and chattels pillaged by the swarm of camp followers, male and female, who straggled in the army's train. It was then that the inhabitants began to mutter about "the Cornwallis Road," and the name became firmly fixed through common usage as yet another tessera in the mosaic of local tradition.

After the Battle of Guilford Courthouse was concluded and the world turned upside down at Yorktown, the tide of loyalist-patriot rancor gradually ebbed, and the old road once again bore the traffic of rural tranquillity. Dusty and rutted in summer, frozen and rutted in winter, and a glutinous gumbo the rest of the time, it lay quietly outside the mainstream of events for eighty-four years until, in April of 1865, it again found itself briefly a minor artery in the throbbing corpus of organized violence. After the Battle of Bentonville on March 16 of that year, General Johnston and his tattered and weary Confederate army retreated north to Hillsborough. Once again foot soldiers trudged, wagons creaked, caissons rumbled, and drivers swore on the Cornwallis Road. Sherman moved to occupy Raleigh and sent his advance to Durham Station. It was to be the final face-off of the blue and gray. Events moved swiftly. Lee surrendered at Appomattox on April 9; Lincoln was assassinated on April 14; and negotiations for the final Confederate surrender began on Easter Monday, April 17.

The site was the Bennet farmhouse, a point midway between the picket lines of the two opposing armies and today only four miles as that linear fowl, the crow, flies from what is now Two-Moon Pond. On April 26, the last Confederate army in the field surrendered, and the long, bitter agony was over. The battle flags were furled, and the armies, if not the enmity, melted away. With the settling dust the old road sank back into bucolic torpor and so remained for more than a century.

When we took up residence at Two-Moon Pond in the early 1960s, the portion of Cornwallis Road we live on was still its old bibulous self. It was now in the county's care, but it was treated as a kind of alcoholic uncle that one keeps in the upstairs back bedroom. Every now and then a truck would spread gravel on parts of its weathered surface and a scraper would be on its heels to push the top dressing to the sides. After a few years of this regimen, the old road had the best-graveled ditches for miles around. It took it all in stride, however, and played its little foxy pranks in retaliation against the newfangled autos—chewing up a few radial tires before breakfast, for instance, or having its wheel-flung rocks smash fist-size holes in gas tanks.

But despite its crotchets and foibles, there were times in the starlit silences of night when, lying pale between the towering palisades of pines, it gave us some sense of our place in time, and we grew attached to it. Here some little rivulets of history ran—a tangible track of memory which we were loath to lose.

But Progress, that brassy bitch, has little use for the vaporings of Romanticism. In the early '70s men with stakes and posts and tripods appeared. Scarlet ribbons began fluttering from judiciously placed markers—plastic autumnal harbingers of what was to be the interminable winter of our discontent.

It was not long before they came: the great, snorting, canary-yellow, diesel-fed dinosaurs. They did not eat; they rooted and tore. What was high was lowered, what sagged was raised, the rough places were made plain and the crooked straight. Down came the big green pines and the huge, ancient oak on the hill by the roadside with a hollow in its trunk one could stand erect in. Gone also were the wild azaleas, dogwoods, and redbuds, the muscadine vines, and the fringe trees. Then large, stinking, black beetles came and laid a smooth, tarry track on the raw earth, and the reformation was complete. Order and efficiency had shown nature the error of its ways, and Tryon's old road, born again and cold sober, was ready to march in lockstep with modern society.

Naturally, it wasn't long before people came, and houses, buses, trucks, semis, motorcycles, passenger cars—and, of course, trouble in the form of vandalism, housebreaking, thievery, trash, and speeding violations, not to mention potholes and crumbling pavement at a time when road maintenance costs are rising and highway funds are short. But many feel that this is a small price to pay for less dust and easier driving.

As a memento of things as they were, though, we have a ten-foot fringe tree which we snatched as a pencil-thin sapling from the path of the steel-jawed saurians and transplanted in the yard. For this effort it rewards us each spring with its blooms—a large, white, puffy cloud of fragrant froth.

## XVIII

# The Dead of Winter

WATCH IT, BOY! THEY'VE GOT A FIX ON YOU."
There was another low, irregular series of hoots
from the female great horned owl in the post oak a hundred
feet to the east and a higher-pitched reply from the male
nearby, but neither my remark nor the ominous signals
from the owls seemed to disturb the blasé rabbit. It had
long since accepted me as a harmless domestic biped and
went on nibbling whatever it had found in the rime-stiff
grass under the bright mercury-vapor night light.

Suppressing a shiver in that biting January dawn, I

hunched my warm coat collar closer to the nape of my neck and resumed my stiff-legged stumping down the causeway to retrieve the morning paper. Seeing me move, the rabbit decided to call it quits for the night and loped leisurely off to disappear in a patch of ivy near the big juniper. The owls, their quarry gone, fell silent.

The rabbit was the last of three who had cavorted and lollygagged around our place during the past summer and autumn. One had fallen victim to a passing vehicle, and I had found the other dead by a pyracantha with a dime-sized warble fly hole in its left flank. As for the survivor, it appeared that its number was up as well, particularly if it persisted in feeding in a brightly illuminated patch of open lawn with great horned owls in the offing.

But the owls never got a second chance. I found the rabbit under a chestnut tree the following morning, neatly decapitated, the top of its skull trepanned with surgical precision, and the brains consumed. This was weasel work. That savage but meticulous killer goes straight for the neck, drinks the blood, eats the brains, and, unlike owls or other predators, leaves not so much as an unattached tuft of fur or a spot of gore behind.

The heart of winter is a bitter, bleak, uncharitable place for warm-blooded wild creatures. Most of the seeds and green growth are gone, the ponds are frozen, the earth iron-hard. Now, under the lash of necessity, predators are forced to even greater efforts and their victims to hunger-driven heedlessness. The kingfisher, barred from the pond surface by a sheet of ice, must now seek out the shallow, spring-fed rills of moving water and make do with what little it can find. The great blue heron, on the other hand, is more resourceful. I was dumbfounded one cold winter day to see a big, gawky spindleshanks attempt a landing thirty feet outside our front window on our ice-locked pond. "No, no! It's slippery, you fool. Come down on land or you'll crash in flames," I muttered to myself, only to have the heron come to rest on the glassy surface as gently as a wisp of thistledown and begin its stately promenade along the dam.

I considered this an exercise in utter futility, for the heron did not have a prayer of catching a fish through two inches of ice. But once again I was wrong, for it was not concerned with the glazed pond surface but rather was eyeballing the ivy-covered dam face with close attention. Suddenly it stopped and slowly extended its neck until, with a sudden thrust and withdrawal, it extracted a small, dark, struggling form, which was vigorously shaken before it began its last dark journey down that long gullet. It was then that I remembered: voles winter over in the ivy. That heron had a feasible plan from the outset, and there would be at least one less rodent in my garden next spring.

With the advent of autumn, the red-tailed, red-shouldered, sharp-shinned, and marsh hawks return to our immediate area, and their appearance is heralded by the ubiquitous blue jays, who voice a cry imitating the "kee-you" of the red-shouldered hawk.

But why do they warn of the red-shouldered hawk, whose diet, like those of the marsh and red-tailed hawks, consists mainly of rodents, reptiles, and amphibians, rather than sound the call of that swift and deadly scourge of the songbirds at our feeder, the sharp-shin? It may be that "kee-you" is more frequently heard or easier to imitate, but in any event it is blue jayese for "hawk."

But even the sharp-eyed but gluttonous jays can be caught napping now and then, and often, as I sit at the kitchen picture window warming my palms with a cup of hot coffee, dozens of birds at the feeder will suddenly disappear as though expunged by a huge eraser. Then I have only to stoop and squint under the awning overhang to see a sharp-shin or two in a nearby tree, looking for stragglers and biding their time. On other occasions this small accipiter will thread its way swiftly through the orchard-size trees to slash like a scimitar through the feeding area and even press, full tilt with talons at the ready, into the bare, pliable branches of a bush where a straggler has taken refuge.

One winter afternoon we were alerted by a jarring thud from the kitchen and rushed to the picture window to find a sharp-shin lying stunned in the grass beneath it. It might have been suckered into an awkward maneuver by a smaller, more agile bird and wound up crashing into a sheet of glass which reflected the open field to its rear. As our forms impinged on its addled wits, it pulled itself together and took off, leaving behind on the glass the dusty, cruciform image of its head, neck, breast and wings as evidence of its incautious foray.

A sharpie's swiftness is exceeded only by its tenacity. We have seen one come to rest on an abelia hedge, peer down intently through the twigs for suspected prey and, still unconvinced, descend to the ground to scrutinize the lower branches more carefully. As a matter of fact, its ability to hunt on foot seems, at this writing, to have gone largely unnoticed, and yet it appears to be one of the bird's most successful ploys. In one instance a sweeping attack scattered the feeding birds, one of which took shelter in the low meadow grass. To my surprise, the hawk landed a short distance away and began slowly quartering the area on foot. When its prey broke cover, the sharp-shin took off and, with a furious burst of speed, made the kill after traversing only thirty feet. Obviously, persistence and speed make a lethal combination.

A less fortunate predator, a gray fox, first came to my attention when I sighted it one night in silhouette against the night light as it trotted down the causeway and melted as silently as its own shadow into the adjacent ravine. I spotted it again a few mornings later as it came pelting down a ditch, pursuer or pursued, to vanish in a thicket. When it appeared again, it was a headless, drawn, flayed carcass draped over a roadside fence post. The head, fur, and tail had undoubtedly gone to a taxidermist or furrier, and the display was intended as a warning to other foxes to mend their thievish ways; but I suspect, since a chicken or a suckling pig still disappears now and then, that it deterred the foxes no more effectively than a human head on a pike inhibited the pirates and brigands in humanity's recent past.

And so the endless round of birth, predation, and death continues, and in response to the age-old question, "Is Nature cruel?" one need only glance at the morning paper and ask, "Compared with what?"

## XIX

# Of Cabbages and Kings

JANUARY, DEEP WINTER, IS A TIME OF RECORD-breaking cold. Earth and water are rock-hard, and the north wind, like a famished timber wolf, snuffles around the crannies of the door and nips at my nape with a rimy muzzle when I venture out. Nothing stirs but the birds and an occasional dead leaf, wind-harried, which scuttles like a crippled crab toward some haven in the hedgerow. The landscape of somber browns and greens is brightened only by intermittent gleams of the sun on ice and the holly berries which glow like little embers in the dark foliage.

Gone is the Christmas candle-shine and the bittersweet of "Auld Lang Syne." The mailbox offers no more greetings from old friends—only throwaways, bills, and a form from the tax man reminding me that since I have picked clean the bones of my Yuletide turkey, it is now his turn to pick mine. It is, in short, the time of cabin fever and the "wormies," of grouchy mornings and restless afternoons when cozy has become stuffy and relaxation tedium.

But then, one day, I hear again the bronchitic heaving of the mail truck and find in the box among the sweepstake offers, coupons, and other dubious solicitations something to buoy the spirit and raise the sap: a seed catalog. Now here indeed is such stuff as one may make dreams of. There on the cover is pictured a magnificent clutch of improbably gorgeous tomatoes, while inside are offerings of plumper, firmer radishes, earlier, more tender broccoli, new, mosaic-resistant snap beans, and some formidable pole limas. And it's not come a moment too soon, I suddenly realize, since February fifteenth, the time for planting green peas and potatoes, is only a month away. I stuff another log into the wood stove and, catalog in hand, settle back into an easy chair. Well, let's see here now!

I have often wondered what there is about that thirty-by-thirty-foot plot of fertile, friable earth and the things growing on it that attracts me often to the point of total preoccupation. There are the fruits of my labor, of course, and a freezer full of prime produce at the season's end is no trifling thing, but I've come to realize that there is more to it than that. Here on this bit of ground I can play the benevolent despot, a suzerain, subject only to the weather, who governs in such a way that the plants in my charge may flourish and bear, unimpeded, to the fullest of their several capacities, creating in so doing a little, pip-squeak Utopia in an otherwise imperfect world.

Man, in the monumental conceit of his species, often describes the faulty character and actions of his fellows by such erroneous references to others of the animal kingdom as filthy swine, jive turkey, damned jackass, and so on. When referring to humans who are simply oblivious or otiose, though, he invariably turns to plants and will describe an indolent, dull-witted lout as "vegetating" and a person in a state of coma as "just a vegetable."

These are pretty hard lines when applied to a group of living things which strive to their utmost to fulfill their purpose in the scheme of things, often under highly adverse circumstances. What man, in his hubris, is getting at, of course, is the fact that plants do not possess that magnificent crowning glory of *homo sapiens*, the human cerebrum, which, he claims, makes him superior to all things on earth and just a little lower than the angels.

This immensely gratifying contention is, naturally, a great comfort to us all, but consider the advantage which accrues to the vegetables through their lack of cogitative globs. The pea vine, for example, does not shrivel in bitterness over the spurious notion that it could bear pomegranates if given a chance. The zucchini's green does not reflect envy of the more flamboyant tomato, nor did that stowaway cauliflower with its brainlike florescence which cropped up among my Brussels sprouts aspire to public office, although if it had and the campaign had been properly run and financed, it would probably have been elecrnd. And no bad thing necessarily, since we certainly have done worse.

No need to patronize or feel contempt for the vegetables, then, simply because they lack a human brain, which is, after all, for far too many people mainly a kind of manufactory for the production and justification or even ennoblement of everything from specious rubbish to utter bestiality.

And so, warmed by the thought that soon the coursing hounds of spring and not the wolf will be whiffling around my stoop, I sit by the stove late on a cold winter afternoon with the setting sun burning like a balefire among the bare trees on the ridge and plan once again, in these vexatious times, the establishment, however ephemeral, of yet another green and peaceable kingdom.

XX

# Early One Morning

SOMEWHERE AROUND THREE A.M., AFTER SOME ITCHY, sheet-tangling, pillow-thumping, wide-eyed hours, I had finally slipped off into fitful sleep when I became fuzzily aware of a faint thumping on the rickety portal of my consciousness. I gathered together such of my faculties as were in working order and tried to focus my attention. Silence. Giving a grateful sigh and a sharp rap on the knuckles to my imagination, I sank back on my pillow.

Thump, thump, thump! A faint, ambiguous, apologetic sort of rap as though the perpetrator was trying to wake someone without disturbing anybody. Who could it be, I wondered. That old, absent-minded klutz who accidentally cast his rod and reel into the pond last week? Hardly. He always announces his presence with the same thunderous pounding as the statue of the Commandant in *Don Giovanni*. Vexed and befuddled, I sent my feet off in search of slippers while I groped for and put on what fortunately proved to be a bathrobe and finally lurched in the direction of the back door.

There in the dimness stood a young man who was house-sitting while our neighbors were away on an extended vacation. He had managed, it seemed, to lock himself out and could he use the phone to call someone who had a key? With all the amiable cordiality of a horned viper I bade him enter and stood sullenly by while he made his call and departed.

What was he doing out at such an hour anyway? He didn't say, and I didn't ask for fear that, like most young people today, he would tell me, and more, possibly, than I wanted to know.

So there I stood, like Kathleen Mavourneen with the gray dawn breaking, wondering what my next move should be.

I should explain at this point that I have two alter egos, each antipathetic to the other, who vie for my attention. I've never actually met them face to face, you understand, but only catch glimpses of them now and then out of the corner of my mind's eye. One is Mr. Mañana, a genial, easygoing sort with heavy-lidded eyes and a gentle smile who always appears at my elbow when a job of work appears unavoidable. In soft, well-modulated tones he invariably points out that it is either too hot, too wet, too windy, too cold, too dry, or too late in the day or season for the task at hand. He is also sure to mention that it looks like rain or that the chore would be much easier if I put it off until I had obtained a particular tool. All in all, he's comfortable to have around, and we get along famously together.

Not so Mrs. Doody. Dressed in a high-necked, ankle-length, black bombazine, her gray hair skinned back into a tight little bun, and her cold, blue eyes peering through steel-rimmed spectacles which perch on the end of a straight, narrow beak of a nose, she is quick to give me the edge of her sharp-honed tongue when she catches me malingering. Naturally, she wouldn't give two cents for the likes of Mr. Mañana and treats him with thin-lipped, icy disdain. I try to avoid her if at all possible, but she always finds me out. As she has repeatedly said, she can read me like a book.

Now Mr. Mañana in view of my dilemma would have suggested that I go back to bed, but he, of course, was fast asleep himself. Mrs. Doody, unfortunately, was up and full of ideas for improving each shining hour. It was the same old spiel with variations.

"Land sakes, you lazy lout," she nattered, "what could be a better time to pick vegetables, pull weeds, thin the onions, cut brush, and edge the flower bed than the cool of the morning when the lark's on the wing and the snail's on the thorn like that poet feller says. Today'll be another scorcher, you know. Besides, the good Lord sent a fine rain yesterday so you needn't waste time watering."

There were a lot of inaccuracies in that. No lark was stirring at that hour, and if the snail was on anything it was on my lettuce. As for the "fine" rain, I could have pointed out that it was a by-blow of a storm that had shredded three million dollars worth of standing tobacco in the next county. But I was not about to argue theology or anything else with her at that time in the morning.

She was right about two things, though: it was cool right then, and the day would be another scorcher.

With all deliberate, fumbling speed I performed a few ablutions and dressed. I then charred two rashers of bacon, carbonized a muffin, brought what was left of the previous night's coffee to a rolling boil and, with reluctance, consumed the lot while glancing at the morning paper to activate my spleen. So sustained and aroused, I was ready, bucket in hand, to venture into the mauve-gray, dew-pearled morning and reap the fruits of my honest toil.

The morning was dew-pearled all right, and while the air was cool enough, the humidity was sky-high. By the time I got to the garden my feet were squelching in my shoes, and I felt as though I were swathed in wet felt. But no matter, the string beans awaited, and I was up and doing.

There were plenty of beans, but there was something else as well that rang no joybells in my heart. Some of the leaves had begun to yellow and crinkle, and some pods had assumed the telltale sickle shape that indicated that a mosaic infestation had struck again—and on a resistant variety, too! Apparently there's no hope of avoiding it, spray and rake as I will. Some members of Masochists International will be quick to point out that picking beans when they are wet tends to spread the infection. This is undoubtedly true, but it should be noted that when they are sufficiently dry, the sun is usually hot enough to peel the hide off an alligator, and I have no intention of cooking myself like a fritter over a measly virus, particularly when aphids are the prime distributors after all.

With the beans picked, I drifted toward the zucchinis—two hills of two vines each. One vine bore a nice plump squash, but something was wrong with the other hill. Both plants had looked puny the day before, and I had laid it to the heat and dry weather; but now, after an inch and a half of rain, the leaves still hung like ragged, green dishrags. The borers, it seemed, had come to call. Regretfully, I jerked up the vines and made a lateral incision in each stalk with my knife. There they were, obscenely fat, coffin-worm white, and greedily boring away, having already reduced several inches of each vine's center to brown mush. With a few deft strokes I slit their weasands and threw the vegetation on the mulch pile. With my anticipated zucchini harvest reduced in a twinkling by fifty percent, I planted a new hill immediately and then dusted every *Cucurbita* in sight.

By now the sky had acquired a milky brightness as the sun tried to pierce the overcast. Down the road beyond the pond a lone, obviously overweight jogger wheezed by in agonized atonement for his gastronomical indiscretions—the first human I'd seen since I was summarily awakened. I moved on to check the bell peppers and found nothing ready to be picked but a large, succulent, squirmy tomato hornworm which seemed to have gotten its signals crossed and missed my tomatoes by a country mile. Its droppings, resembling tiny, squat replicas of pineapple-type hand grenades, had collected on a lower leaf and had given it away. Time was when, as a child, I would have caged and fed it in anticipation of the cocoon, pupation, and the ultimate, miraculous emergence of the adult. But many of childhood's miracles have become an adult's destructive nuisances, their wonder past. I sent it the way of the borers.

The overcast had thinned, and I became aware of an almost tangible weight of hot sunshine bearing down as I moved to the tomatoes. A half-dozen were partially ripe, but it seemed that I had had more company. Three of the six had ragged holes chewed in them. So we're back to that, are we? Let a tomato show a hint of pink, and in come the meadow voles. Little Danny Meadow Mouse, my eye! They may be cow'rin, tim'rous beasties to some, but to me their arrogance and guile are boundless. With determined tread and outthrust jaw I marched off to the shed for the rodent pellets, which, in appropriate containers, I placed among the tomato vines together with small bowls of water. I provide the latter not out of solicitude but rather as a second line of defense. The pellets, when ingested, raise the rodents' thirst, and if no water is available, they'll chew up anything juicy near at hand.

I was beginning to feel frustrated. There were many things still to be done, the temperature was rising, and I was constantly being shunted off course by the unexpected. On the way to the house with my bucket of slim pickings I noticed that a congregation of tent caterpillars had decided to hold a revival meeting on one of the lower branches of a black walnut tree, so I detoured long enough to roll them up in their own big top and gave them a thorough stomping. Now, at last, for the weeds!

There was no doubt about it—it was really getting hot. I had just begun prying a well-established pokeweed root out of some hard-packed soil when I happened to glance at the raspberry patch. The berries were long gone, but the tip of every seven-foot cane was bearing a cluster of rounded, iridescent objects which glistened in the sun. Japanese beetles! Here it was, July 28, and they were still hanging around. Their lease was to have expired in three days, and they should have been home packing. They had cut a wide swath this year beginning with the fox grapes and Virginia creepers, which pained me not at all, but then they went on to devour my roses and blackberries, and that drew blood. If the beetles had been blackberries, I'd now be up to my armpits in jam. As it was, I got none.

I am leery of using traps for them as I suspect that they

may lure more beetles to an area than they kill. My observation has been that an infestation at a given point usually begins with the arrival of a nucleus of one or two that I suspect are female. They seem to lure a cluster of others to them, and soon a gluttonous and sexual orgy is in full swing with the females munching merrily away while bestrode.

I don't know what natural enemies the Japanese beetles have other than milky spore. Birds do not seem to fancy them at all, although a mockingbird will almost turn itself inside out to snatch a big, droning, green June beetle on the wing. The only creatures I know that consume them with relish are bluegills, which goozle them like gumdrops when they are offered as bait, but that does not help my garden one bit.

In disgust I sloped off once again to the shed for the applicator and gave the raspberry patch a thorough dusting. The yard and garden were bathed in searing golden sunlight now, and the muggy, blowtorch breeze only made matters worse. Perspiration had soaked the sweatband of my terry-cloth hat and was streaming over my glasses in a blinding cascade.

I checked the thermometer. Eighty-nine soggy degrees in the shade and rising. Time to hang it up and join my wife for a cup of fresh coffee, I thought, and I fancied I saw the newly risen Mr. Mañana smile and murmur, "A wise decision. Another hour of this and you'd shrivel like a prune. Anyway, those weeds and onions and such— they'll still be there tomorrow."

Fine words and fitly spoken. Good old Mr. Mañana. As for Mrs. Doody, not a peep out of her. For once she knew when to keep her mouth shut.

XXI

# Fishing Down the Sun

BY EARLY SEPTEMBER SUMMER HAS GONE SEEDY AND out at the elbows. The green raiment of June, fresh, crisp, and bandbox new has become, under the glare of the July and August sun and the depredations of cutting, chewing, mining, and piercing insects, a dusty, worn, and tattered garment. The days now are becoming noticeably shorter, the evenings cooler, and here and there, in the magic sidelight of a late-season sundown, clouds of whining midges gyrate in an aerial melee.

It is such Lilliputian creatures as these which serve as

the meat and potatoes for my small bass and for bluegills of any size, and as these insects suddenly hatch from the water in their millions, they can set off a feeding frenzy on the part of the fish that puts the entire pond surface into a state of agitation.

The first to notice are the wheeling swallows (and, on one occasion, a veritable blizzard of purple martins), which begin circling over the pond's face to snatch the emerging insects off the surface. This action invariably engages the attention of the fish, and it is not long before the slurpy smacking of feeding bluegills engages mine. Now, with work and dinner over, it's time for my fly rod and tiny yellow popping bug, for this will probably go on until dark.

I strip off some line, flick a few false casts for extra yardage, and cast out. The popper zips through the flight of birds and hits the water. Slurp! The line snaps taut as I strike and bring a protesting bluegill in by hand retrieval. In a moment the fish is unhooked and in the wire mesh basket. I'm ready for another cast.

As the fishing gets hot and heavy and the sun sinks lower, the swallows begin to thin out and are ultimately replaced by a half-dozen nighthawks. Goatsuckers, people used to call them in the ridiculous belief that they subsisted by sucking milk from goats' teats. I try to visualize this bizarre procedure and decide that no nanny would ever hold still for it. Slurp! Another fish, and I stop to count my catch. Seventeen keepers in twenty-three minutes. A good mess, but the feeding is slacking off.

As the last rays of sunset cast their attenuated shadows and the action slows, I have time between strikes to look around. The swifts, I notice, are dropping one by one into our chimney. Once these birds have started on their long migration to Peru, I must remember to call the sweep.

No more encrusted flues for me when the wood stove season begins.

Now twilight, and all but one of the nighthawks has departed as the first bat appears. I glance at the mercury vapor night-watch light by the shed. Sure enough, it's on. The photoelectric cell which triggers the light and the photorecorder in the bats' brains are, in this case, responsive to precisely the same degree of diminishing brightness. Another bat appears, then two more. One is irked by the nighthawk's presence and drives it off. Another veers to take a radar reading of my airborne popping bug and evidently does not like the looks of the blip, for it shrewdly passes it up. A lucky thing for me too. Reeling in a pain-maddened, flying bat in the gathering dusk is not exactly my idea of fishing.

How did we come to refer to addlepated people as batty or as having bats in their belfries anyway, I wonder. No doubt our forebears, those respected repositories of the wisdom of the ages, could detect no reasonable pattern in the bats' irregular and seemingly aimless blunderings and so used their name to describe the condition and behavior of the flitterwitted. Bats, they also insisted, like nothing better than to get entangled in one's hair—an activity no self-respecting bat would dream of engaging in. Fortunately, we now know how finely tuned and proficient bats are at making ends meet, and to be called batty should by now be considered a compliment. Being loony, of course, is something else again. Everyone knows that loons are crazy. And coots too—particularly old ones!

Slurp! A hefty fish this time, for my thin leader is as taut as a fiddle's E-string. The fish is trying to keep itself broadside to the direction of pull and, at the last moment before landing, executes a frantic flurry of pinwheels. Out and into the basket it goes.

# TWO-MOON POND

The air is cool on my back now as it slides gently down the sloping meadow to the pond. As it reaches the water, pillars of mist begin to form and glide slowly across the surface like files of gray-cowled friars moving silently to evensong. Darkness deepens, the stars appear, and, as if on cue, a distant bird repeatedly demands that poor Will receive yet another whipping.

The pond is silent now, and under a rising, gibbous moon, with my tackle secured and twenty-two fish in the basket, I trudge back, pleasantly weary, to the house and the comfort of my easy chair.

# XXII

# *Postludium*

AT THIS WRITING IT HAS BEEN ALMOST TWENTY YEARS since we forsook the dubious advantages of city life for a rural residence. Time, place, and experience have wrought their changes in us—mostly, we hope, for the better. We have learned a little something about the importance of patience, the futility of arguing with the inevitable, the appreciation of small benefits, and the immutable law that each living thing must die so that another may live. We have endured no physical hardships whatever but acquired in our brief stints in garden, field, and woodlot a profounder respect for those who, in the past, provided for themselves and their families with little but an axe, a rifle, a shovel, and a plow. All in all, it's been a good school and, mercifully, not a dear one.

Most of the lessons I have learned have been education in its true sense—the drawing out of things I already knew but ignored and things I could easily have figured out if I had taken the trouble to use my head. The listing of them might well serve as an appendix to the Decalogue and save the more knuckle-headed of God's chillun a lot of trouble and inconvenience, although, people being what they are, they probably wouldn't pay attention to these either. I list a few:

1. Thou shalt not pour slops uphill.
2. Thou shalt not shovel manure into the wind.
3. Thou shalt not stand around under a heavily laden black walnut tree on windy October days.
4. Thou shalt not straddle a felled sapling and, grasping the axe handle near the head, employ it as an hatchet for the lopping of branches; for, if thou dost, then will the near end of the handle surely rise and smite thee such a blow as thou wilt long remember.

The list is a long one, and it would be helpful if the various items could somehow be retained in racial memory, but unfortunately, they are things which must be relearned by each successive generation.

We have found Nature to be capricious, completely impersonal, often rigorous, and much inclined to grant fools short shrift. To have spent two decades in close association with this froward hussy and to have come through it relatively unscathed says something for our adaptability and circumspection.

But, as we all know, Nature has her milder and more

generous side, and now and then she will disburse a few gratuities, a handful or two of lagniappe strewn here and there for those willing to stoop or reach for it. Among these are the wild strawberries which she scatters in the springtime fields and ditches to be followed shortly in the hedgerows by glistening blackberries and wild black cherries. Autumn brings the purple-orange persimmons and blue-black muscadines and, finally, an abundance of black walnuts.

It was over these last obdurate, rock-hard rascals that I achieved a small victory of sorts. The hulling and drying were no problem, and I soon grew skillful enough with a hammer to crack them into quarters without mushing up my fingers. The real problem was extracting the meats from the sections of shell—a picky-picky, crumby business which was not worth the effort. It then occurred to me that if I could not remove the meat from the shell, could I remove the shell from the meat? I discarded the nutpick and got out a small pair of wire-cutters—six-inch nippers—and began snipping at the edges of the shells. After a few false starts I got the hang of it; the shells split and came away easily, and in less than two hours I had a brimming cup of large black walnut chunks which could either be used as is or ground up. During the following winter I cracked more than five gallons of meats, averaging a pint an evening.

But this, for me, shows uncommon zeal and dedication. I am at heart a lotus-eater, I suppose, and am much governed by inertia in that when I am at rest I tend to remain so and when in motion am easily diverted or brought to a halt by any irregularity in my path. A mountain of unfinished chores will sometimes send me into feverish spasms of activity, but these usually abate when I've reduced it to the point where I can see over the top when standing on tiptoe. Naturally, what I accomplish depends entirely on which of my imaginary alter egos prevails at any given moment, the lackadaisical Mr. Mañana or the prickly, bodkin-tongued Mrs. Doody, although the former, understandably, has the edge.

Despite the cajolery of my indolent adviser, things do seem to get done eventually, and I think I have discharged the obligations of my temporary stewardship of this bit of land and pressed it to fill our needs without resorting to the gross abuses so much of our earth is subjected to. This area has, after all, supported man for thousands of years and, despite his occupancy, is none the worse for it.

That I had ancient predecessors was made plain to me when I started digging a garden plot behind the lean-to. Beneath the top dressing of broken glass and crockery and a miscellany of rusted rubbish, at one spade depth below the surface, I found the Stone Age—two flint points, one of which I identified as a stemmed point (Late Woodland, circa 1000 A.D.) and the other as a Savannah River point (circa 2000 B.C.). To this spot above the ravine with its spring of cool, sweet water they came, those people of a simpler time. They had their brief hours in the sun and then departed, and in their passing left the good land to posterity much as they found it.

What will our legacy be, I wonder. Four millennia from now will there be a green, peaceful, prosperous earth ringed with a jeweled girdle of satellite colonies? Or will some truly sapient beings one day stumble on our ruins, sift our toxic rubble, and say, "Here was *Homo shlemieliens*; he created far more problems than he solved"?